Starrs

The New York
Public Library®
GUIDE *to*
READING
GROUPS

❧

The New York Public Library®

GUIDE *to* READING GROUPS

∾

Rollene Saal

CROWN TRADE PAPERBACKS
NEW YORK

For my Dear Ones
who always wanted one more story
Theodora, Matthew, Drusilla, Albert

༽

Copyright © 1995 by The New York Public Library®
and Rollene Saal

Published by Crown Publishers, Inc., in hardcover and by Crown Trade Paperbacks in
paperback, 201 East 50th Street, New York,
New York 10022. Member of the Crown Publishing Group.
Random House, Inc., New York, Toronto, London, Sydney, Auckland

Crown and Crown Trade Paperbacks are trademarks of Crown Publishers, Inc.
Manufactured in the United States of America

Library of Congress Cataloging-in-Publication Data
Saal, Rollene.
The New York Public Library guide to reading groups / by Rollene Saal.
p.   cm.
I. Group reading—United States.   I. New York Public Library.   II. Title.
LC6615.S22   1995   94-44510
CIP

ISBN 0-517-88357-0 (pbk.)
0-517-70010-7
10 9 8 7 6 5 4 3 2 1
First Edition

Contents

∾

THE BOOKLISTS

Acknowledgments

People who read books like to talk about them, so it was no real surprise that countless members of reading groups with whom I spoke around the country were generous with their time, with their thoughtful ideas about what made their own groups work, and with the names of other book club people, which added links to the chain. Our conversations invariably ended with an exchange about our favorite books, because readers know that the best present you can give to another reader is the title of an undiscovered book.

Thanks especially to Lauran Posner, Napa, California; Elaine Hanson Raitt, Portola Valley, California; Robilee Deane, St. Helena, California; Lesley Harris, San Francisco, California; Marianna McJimsey, Elaine Yaffe, Colorado Springs, Colorado; Ruth and Arnold Greenfield, Miami, Florida; Katherine McCaughan, Chicago and Hong Kong; Patti Nickell, Lisa Slatten, New Orleans; Penny Zeisler Catzen, Baltimore, Maryland; Richard Howarth, Lisa Pritchard, Oxford, Mississippi; Marilyn Bender, Barbara Harris, Kenneth Lewis, Eden Ross Lipson, Elaine Morris, Patricia Murphy, Jerry Patterson, Elizabeth Robin Spiegel, Susan Zeckendorf, New York City; Lopez Adorno, Hunter College, New York City; Clara Cazzulino, Long Island, New York; Milton Lipson, Sea Cliff, Long Island; Sue Shattuc Raitt, Portland, Oregon; Evelyn Rosen, Philadelphia, Pennsylvania; Elizabeth Glaize Helm, Winchester, Virginia; Charlene Volmer, Mercer Island, Washington.

My thanks to those at The New York Public Library who

always led me in the right direction: Barbara Shapiro, Harriet Gottlieb, Jan Klucevsek, Barbara Bergeron, Cynthia Mustafa, Mary Crown. Thank you as well to Beth Mason who shared information on the Wilton, Connecticut Library's extensive reading programs.

I love continuity, the sense of connection with one's own past, which is why it has been so pleasurable to reconvene with people I have known and worked with at other, earlier times in our lives. This has been a project dear to all our hearts and I thank them from the bottom of mine: Lucia Staniels, my literary agent; Karen Van Westering, who manages the publications program at The New York Public Library; Barbara Greenman, executive editor of GuildAmerica Books; and Betty A. Prashker, my editor at Crown Publishers.

And, finally, thanks to my own reading groups, Booklovers, who are always eager to read the next book.

Foreword

 ❧

"How many a man has dated a new era in his life from the reading of a book," observed Henry David Thoreau in his great work, *Walden*. Indeed, books tend to stand in the readerly life like milestones along an ascending highway. Together, they form a tangible chart of an individual's growth and development, each one a step toward a new understanding of oneself and the world.

While the contemplation of books may have been for Thoreau a solitary act, many people have a strong desire to share the reading experience with other readers. For some, the discussion of a book is an essential aspect of reading it, as though the hours of silent passage demand a return to the realm of verbal exchange. This is quite understandable, for such discussion is invariably a valuable undertaking. In the articulation of thoughts about a book, ideas crystallize, issues are seen in sharper profile, literary characters take on new dimensions. Talking about a book with others is a way to continue reading it in a sense. It allows us to see with new eyes and to hear with different ears.

In their myriad manifestations, reading groups offer individuals a structured outlet for this desire to speak about books. Within a group, readers can focus their opinions and enhance their understanding and gather new perspectives. The group also imparts a social aspect that is not always a part of the reading experience. Many enduring friendships (and very few enmities, I imagine) have undoubtedly been forged in the fires of a reading group discussion.

The support and promotion of adult reading has been a

part of The New York Public Library's work since the early 1900s. Through the sponsorship of these groups the Library found a key way to function as an educational institution for the citizens of New York City, and not merely, as one critic termed it, "a huge slot machine for dispensing fiction." After World War II, the Library's Great Books discussion groups flourished, and since the 1950s, the branch libraries of The New York Public Library have sponsored numerous adult reading groups organized around varying themes.

During 1994–1995, the Library sponsored nineteen reading groups in Manhattan, the Bronx, and Staten Island, involving over 350 participants. These groups are a vital medium through which the Library seeks to instill an appreciation of books and a love of reading in people throughout the city. We have seen the many ways that a library's resources can help bring cohesion to a neighborhood, and reading groups are an important element in the promotion of that sense of community.

Philanthropist Brooke Russell Astor has been a lifelong devotee of reading groups. In an article she wrote for *House & Garden* magazine in 1988, she described her group of the time as follows: "We talked and talked, which is what one wants in a reading group. There is no point in reading if you do not form opinions. The whole idea is to take a look at life through books and then to have the fun of discussing them with other people."

The essence of it is that simple: to learn and to enjoy. The reading group facilitates that, and this volume helps guide the creation of a productive and harmonious group. There is no magic formula, of course. Like good books themselves, each group is unique. But there are certain important steps that can be taken to ensure a good, balanced group. In the pages that follow, Rollene Saal provides clear and practical advice for those forming groups and for those who wish to add new life to existing groups. Of course, one of the key factors is the choice of books for the group. The reading lists included here draw on the Library's holdings and include annotations on the selections made. They are replete with titles that will assuredly spark memorable and meaningful discussions.

If, in the silent and personal act of reading, a part of the world is somehow given from one person to another—from writer to reader—then the reading group is a way for the reader to give it back to the world. Through discussion, the solitary act of reading becomes a process of exchange and shared reading. In this way, books can be magnets for bringing people together, even as they propel individuals into new areas of personal understanding and growth.

Dr. Paul LeClerc
President
The New York Public Library

~

READING
GROUPS

~

HOW IT
ALL BEGAN

❧

I had never belonged to a reading group, nor had I ever been a teacher, so when an old college friend called to ask if I would like to lead a reading group of some of her friends, I promptly said no.

"But you like books," she said. "Doesn't everyone?" I dodged. "You also especially like 19th-century books," she pursued, "and those are exactly the kind of novels that my friends want to read together. Think about it," she said, "and draw up a list of some of your favorites."

I did think about it. I thought about it at night as I was brushing my teeth, as I got into bed, in that early morning reverie between sleeping and awakening, on the treadmill at the gym, when I was waiting for the bus, and even when I was reading. I thought about where a book group should begin reading.

Did they plunge right into the storm of the 19th century with Charlotte Brontë? That would catch their attention! Or should they begin more decorously with Jane Austen or should we—because by this time, in my mind, it was no longer "they" but "we" who would be off on a literary journey together.

Should we begin properly with the earliest writings that were called novels? That would mean going back to the 18th century to start perhaps with Samuel Richardson or Tobias Smollett or Henry Fielding and read about the besieged Pamela or the boisterous Tom Jones. Or maybe we shouldn't be so parochially English, or even so Western. Perhaps we should go back, way back, to 11th-century Japan and *The Tale of Genji*, where best-sellers really got going. No, I quickly put that aside as something that didn't feel right—and there, right there, that decision marked an important furthering of my conception both of what a reading group is all about and also of what it is not.

A reading group is not school. Books do not have to follow one another in logical or chronological order. There are no tests and no grades. The only homework is to read the book to which we have committed our attention. There doesn't have to be a syllabus, a schedule, or even continuity among the books. Many successful groups skip blithely from Edith Wharton's *The Age of Innocence* to E. Annie Proulx's *The Shipping News*. For them, each reading group session is complete unto itself, concentrated upon the book at hand without too many concerns about how it fits into the overall literary scheme of things.

If we did begin with Jane Austen, which was where my heart was leaning, which one of her richly satisfying novels would be our introduction to the sumptuous dinner before us? Should we start out with a novel as familiar and beloved as *Pride and Prejudice*? What about the youthful high spirits of *Sense and Sensibility*? In my mind, I made some calculations about the group of women as they had been described to me. Most of them had known each other for many years, and all had husbands, grown children, and a top-drawer, if long ago, college education, which meant that they had read most of the classic novels in some mostly forgotten college English survey class.

All that turned out to be true, but we also discovered, along the way, that having read a book back in school days did not necessarily disqualify it for inclusion on our current booklists. That was only one of the discoveries we made. But more about those discoveries later.

What I actually chose as the first book our group, which we named Booklovers, would read was Jane Austen's *Persuasion*, the novel in which a "mature" heroine (those were the days when a 28-year-old woman was assigned to eternal maidenhood) gets a second chance at love. It was a novel none of the members had read, which seemed important because only later did we discover those virtues of re-reading. Most of the other books we read and discussed in that first season we spent together were selected because they were a stretch, a reach out of the ordinary run of that particular author's works. For instance, George Eliot's *Daniel Deronda* and Edith Wharton's *Summer* were not the first books by those authors that one would think of. They were lesser known, lesser-read books that would catch the group's attention.

Now I know that most reading groups don't have to try that hard to find the perfect book, because there are countless books to choose from and many monthly meetings still to come. But back then I was new at it, and it took a while to understand that each book brings something in its own way that is special to the group.

EVERYONE WANTS TO READ... TOGETHER

*A*lthough no one seems to have statistics on how many reading groups are functioning throughout the United States, everyone agrees that some very immense number of people get together on a regular basis to read and discuss books. That's comforting to remember when we are besieged by gloom-and-doom reports announcing the imminent death of the book.

Reading groups themselves aren't new. There has always been some variation on the book group as we know it. People have always wanted to get together to talk about books. In other times and other places, whether it was France of the splendid 18th century or later in the clubs and drawing rooms of 19th-century

London, gentlefolk gathered for conversation about the latest periodicals or books. Women like Mme. de Staël and Lady Mary Wortley Montagu knew the power of the literary salon and often used it to turn social and political acquaintances into friends.

Now, men and women—though reading groups are overwhelmingly populated by women, and we'll talk more about that later—seek out others with whom to share their ideas and feelings and to express them through the medium of books.

E. M. Forster understood this when he wrote in the epigram at the beginning of his novel *Howards End*, "Only connect. . . ." That speaks with such simple eloquence of the yearning that human beings share for connection with one another, the notion that together is better than alone. Sharing one's thoughts in an atmosphere of safety and respect is essential to reading groups. In a successful reading group, members bond with one another; they feel a special closeness from their shared sensibilities and develop a strong feeling of identification with others in the group. When reading group members get together to talk books, they exchange more than their opinions. On a more profound psychological level, they also receive emotional satisfaction from being both nurtured and validated.

"Reading can be a wonderful vehicle to satisfy that yearning to connect," says Dr. Susan Kavaler-Adler, a New York psychoanalyst and author of *The Compulsion to Create*. "Women especially want to share their inner life, but they are often fearful of competition. A reading group provides a safe way of expressing intellectual needs without having to be reminded of school. Here, there is no undue fear about who is doing better or having to compete for grades. Instead, it provides a haven where you can share one's insecurities and put them into more intellectual terms by discussing the characters in a novel instead of oneself."

In her book, Dr. Kavaler-Adler explores modes of creativity in female writers such as Emily and Charlotte Brontë, Sylvia Plath, and Emily Dickinson. "Women writers tend to write about characters who are their alter egos," says Kavaler-Adler, pointing out as examples that the Brontë sisters, Katherine Mansfield, and Virginia Woolf use many fragments of themselves in their fictional characters.

"Women readers can readily identify with these writers and their characters. By commenting upon these fictional people and their relationships, they are able to be more open about how they feel about themselves," notes Kavaler-Adler. "A reading group allows its members indirectly to reveal their own deep feelings."

There are many reasons why reading groups are so popular, and have become increasingly so in recent years. Historically, women especially have enjoyed getting together for conversation, for "visiting," while at the same time excusing the pleasure part of the activity by combining it with some useful work. Whether the justified social activity was a colonial quilting bee or a World War II session of rolling bandages and knitting afghan squares, women have found busy hands a good reason to congregate together. Today, women feel no hesitancy about getting together for intellectual reasons. Reading groups give their members a way to continue to learn. For those who feel the lapses in their formal education, reading groups provide a great way for a catch-up. For the already well educated, reading groups provide a way to sample those books that they never read in college.

Most everyone agrees that if "Good Reading" was not done under some school regimen, then for the most part it never got done. Proust, Joyce, and the Russians are the most frequent victims of neglect and the ones that stir the most guilt feelings among would-be readers. Those books lie moldering on the still-to-be-read list. "I've always wanted to read *War and Peace* but I've never gotten that chunk of free time." "I was so proud when I read Proust's *Combray* in my college French class. I always promised myself that I would read the rest of *Remembrance of Things Past* but of course I never have." Reading groups give their members a chance to catch up, to clean the slate of books they always promised themselves to read and to add new ones.

Many people join book groups because they want to share with others their opinions about what they have read. It's no fun to read a substantive book, or any book for that matter, and not have someone with whom to discuss it. Family members, office workers, husbands and wives, close friends, often do not share the same reading tastes. Can there be a more isolating activity than to read your way through one of the world's classics or to tackle some recent, perhaps enigmatic novel, and then not have anyone to listen to what you have to say about it or, just as important, to answer your questions about what the book was really all about?

Lesley Harris, an attorney in San Francisco, cites Michael Ondaatje's *The English Patient* as a good enough reason for belonging to a reading group. "We really wanted to figure out what those elliptical final chapters were about, and in our discussion we really came to grips with the book. That is very satisfying."

One of the hallmarks of a successful reading group is the

quality of the commitment of its members. They read the book to the last page, attend the monthly meetings religiously, and contribute with enthusiasm to the discussion. They are also often the busiest people around. Though many retired people belong to reading groups, so do actively engaged professionals, who dash to meetings from corporate boardrooms, hospital corridors, and courtrooms. Some of the most involved reading groupers are parents of young children, who take their "night out" as a special occasion.

One explanation for this commitment by otherwise fully occupied people is that the reading group offers an occasion to do something strictly for oneself. It is not of any special benefit for spouse, children, business or profession. Its rewards are strictly selfish. As one Seattle mother of a toddler said, "My reading group is my time. It is just for me and I really value it."

You'd be surprised how many people there are who, if given half a chance, will want to join you. Remember, they don't have to do too many hard things. You're not asking for a lot of the two things most people hold dear: time and money.

GETTING
STARTED

⌒

*I*t isn't all that difficult to start a reading group. That's the beauty of it. You don't even need many people to form a good group. You want to start small and grow to medium-sized. Some successful groups are as small as 6 members or as large as 20, but those are the extremes on both sides. The most favored range for a reading group is from 8 to 12 members. It's always, however, a good idea to have a few more members than you actually need to keep discussion going and lively and representing different points of view. It's good to keep in mind that a few members won't be able to attend any given session and so it's wise to have a somewhat larger group to provide for absences. You also want members who will be agreeable to talking about what they have read, only to the degree, of course, that they choose to do so. They get to do this in a congenial atmosphere, especially since they have one important thing in common: they all, after all, like books.

Who's the Boss?

A group gets started usually because someone wants it. That is, one or two people decide that they would like to belong to a reading group and, not finding an existing one available for them to join, they decide to start their own. In such a case, the group already has a leader or two, in the sense of someone in charge, or at least people who are prepared to set things in motion to form an active reading group. That doesn't mean that once the group is under way, these founders will still be involved in running things.

Groups usually work similarly. Members of reading groups from Seattle to Miami seem to agree upon keeping everything very simple. I have rarely heard of a group with a president or a real slate of officers. Most groups have the lightest possible reins of administration. Once in a while, we hear of a group that has a secretary who keeps track of the books that have been read. Occasionally, someone is designated to send out postcards to remind members about the next meeting. More often than not, no one reminds anyone. It has already been established that the group meets on the last Sunday of the month or the second Tuesday, or whenever. Everyone jots it down on a calendar and that is pretty much that.

What characterizes reading group members—apart from their being smart people who like to talk about books—is how busy they are. Once they have set aside the time for reading, they don't want to devote much energy to the administrative aspects of running a group. They all agree on streamlining everything, from tossing aside customary parliamentary rules that govern other clubs to keeping refreshments simple. Once again, it is the books that count.

Some groups bring in outside leaders and pay them a fee to organize the group, to suggest books that the members would enjoy, and to lead the book discussions. This leader usually brings in background material on the author, comments and reviews, and anything else that may serve to illuminate the general discussion. He or she then takes charge of the discussion so that if any side conversations get started or some dissonance begins to reign, it is easily brought into check.

It shouldn't be difficult to find someone who would be willing to lead a group. Teachers, librarians, and the book reviewer for your local newspaper are all people to whom books are important, and one of them may be the right person to convey the excitement that can inspire a group. Remember, though, no one wants a strict teacher. If the members wanted to be back in school, they would be taking a literature class in an adult education program, rather than showing up at a reading group. In fact, most reading groups do not seek out a teacher, although they may on occasion have some outside authority come and speak to them about a specific book.

But most reading groups don't work with a professional leader or a facilitator. Often the host is the one who introduces the book under discussion. Other groups feel that the host has enough to do in providing the house and the refreshments; they prefer to designate someone else, usually the person who suggested the book in the first place, to offer it to the group.

Dr. Susan Kavaler-Adler, who herself leads several therapy

groups, sees reading groups as an arena where women enjoy great success because they put a high premium on bonding with other women. "They enjoy putting their thoughts and opinions forward and then, by the close of the discussion, to pull it all together in some harmonious closure. Women especially like to find the similarities in their differing ideas and to come to an agreement. They don't need someone to lead them to it. They have a natural feel for consensus."

How to Find Good Members

One of the best ways to get started is to invite three friends who you know like to read to come to your apartment or house to start a reading group. Ask each of them to invite one other person. If that works, you will have a core group of seven, which is a perfectly good place to begin. I used the word "friends" as a starting point, but it often works out even better if you cast a wider net to catch potentially interesting readers. Some great hostess once said that the best parties are those that include friends and strangers. That sounds like good advice for reading groups as well, because a mixture of people who already know one another together with some unfamiliar faces causes that little frisson of excitement and new interest.

Some of the best reading group members come from unlikely sources. Don't just stick to your old college roommate, your bridge partner, the next-door neighbor. Think wider. Your dentist, or the person who works for him/her, that bright person at your local dry cleaner or the pharmacy or your health club with whom you always have such pleasant exchanges, might make a lively group person. Try to see in another context people whom you have enjoyed talking with but with whom you don't have a social relationship. They might make interesting additions to your group, and you'll get to broaden the range of people you know.

Any age works. Don't be age discriminatory. What makes some reading groups very successful is the variety of people in the group. Jerry Patterson, a New York–based author, belongs to a close-knit reading group in Manhattan. Now in its seventh year, the group comprises eight members, four men and four women whose ages sample each decade from the 30s to the 60s. "We each bring something special to our discussion," says Patterson. "After all, we grew up at different times and that brings a real variety of insights into our reading."

WHAT'S THE RIGHT SIZE?

Can a group be too big? Sure, it can. I keep getting back to the notion that a reading group is not a class. If the group gets too large, then the wonderful feelings of spontaneity, that sense that any member can speak up easily, is lost. When you have to raise your hand and wait dutifully to be called upon, then the fun of the reading group starts to lessen. It will feel like back-to-school time. You want to be sure that there can be a ready exchange of opinions, an easy give-and-take of ideas and interpretations, and that the forum isn't so big that people feel uncomfortable about speaking before what may appear to be a large group.

For me and the groups with whom I have worked, any group larger than 20 seems unwieldy. Even that many seems large, because I'm accustomed to groups that meet in each other's houses or apartments, where space limitations say something about how many can fit comfortably in a room. I like the idea that a reading group is really a contemporary extension of the old quilting bee or sewing circle. That in itself means that you want just enough people to sit comfortably in a roomy circle or around a big table.

WHERE ARE THE MEN?

It is a truth universally acknowledged that women dominate reading groups. All kinds of reasons have been offered to explain this phenomenon. One reason that doesn't convince is that men are too busy. Women are now, have always been and will continue to be human beings in full occupancy. They also make great readers. Reading groups are filled with women who juggle their roles as career professionals, working mothers, or mothers with small children and full-time family responsibilities. These are the women who tuck their assigned book into briefcases, diaper bags, or wherever they can stow it, to be pulled out for a few stolen minutes of reading time. No, it's not that women have more leisure time. It must be something else.

One woman commented, not altogether in jest: "Men, my own wonderful husband included, have no friends. At least not in the way that we do. No wonder they can't get a group together!" That may be hyperbolic but it has a germ of truth in that most men don't have the network of support that women build with other women, whether office or playground pals, next-door neighbors, former college roommates, close colleagues, or best friends.

It has been said that men are too competitive to enjoy be-longing to a reading group, in which there are no points to score, no games to win. Most reading groups count it a success when a book discussion consists of differing opinions, some keen conversation about the various points of view, and a resolution that often results in a consensus. Women are good at that. They do not, by and large, enjoy making points by putting down their opponents. In fact, there are no opponents in a reading group, no blue or green team.

Most women members of book groups would certainly welcome more male readers. Groups who do count men among their members remark that they bring a different sensibility, texture, and viewpoint to the discussion.

The First Meeting

There are a few things that should be discussed at your very first meeting. Once you get the housekeeping details agreed upon and out of the way, you'll have a clean slate to move ahead to the books, which is what, after all, you are meeting for anyway.

HOW OFTEN WILL YOU MEET?

Most groups meet once a month. A few groups meet every six weeks. You can determine, according to your own schedules, whether or not you choose to meet during the summer months. Some groups enjoy a two-month summer vacation from meetings, but not from reading. July and August is a good time to read a book that is long enough to need and deserve a summer's reading. My own reading group, Booklovers, read first *War and Peace* and then *Anna Karenina* during two successive summers and everyone was exceptionally pleased at the summer accomplishment. Proust is lying in wait for the next holiday months.

A Few Simple Rules

One of the ways to have a successful group is to set up the rules about when and where early on and stick to them. If you decide to meet at 7 p.m. on the last Wednesday of each month, then no matter whose anniversary it is or what business trip interferes, you must continue with the agreed-upon date. Begin promptly at the set time. Even if people straggle in late for the first couple of meetings, they will soon get the idea that you do start on time. It's important to be respectful of your reading group, and you may be pleasantly surprised when even chronic latecomers begin to firm up their arrival time.

Where Will You Meet?

If you plan to meet at each other's apartments or houses, set up the schedule at the first meeting through the rest of the year. That way, if Mary Alice knows in September that the meeting is at her house on the second Tuesday in May, she won't make an appointment for a periodontal cleaning for that day. It's just a good idea for everyone to be clear, well in advance, who is host and when.

Most often, book groups meet at home and members take turns chairing the meeting. If a member can't invite the group to meet at his/her house—sometimes there is not enough room in an apartment, or too many small children are sleeping or, worse yet, not sleeping—then that person will usually offer to help out with refreshments at someone else's place. The best groups have this kind of informality within the structure so that "housekeeping" problems can be easily worked out.

Sometimes, however, the home route isn't the one that a group chooses to take. Reading groups now meet in an increasingly imaginative array of both public and private places: the library, of course, is a longtime haven of reading groups; schools, churches and synagogues, meeting halls, community and senior citizen centers, and school rooms are also possibilities. In fact, any public place that is free a few hours once a month can serve as a meeting center.

Reading group members have used their imaginations to come up with additional places to hold their meetings. Bookstores have cropped up as popular meeting places. Some bookstores offer, along with the free space, a discount for reading group members on the books that are purchased for group use. From mammoth bookstores such as New York City's blockwide Barnes & Noble and Portland, Oregon's Powell's, to smaller, independent bookstores such as Square Books in Oxford, Mississippi, bookstores seem an increasingly comfortable niche for reading groups.

Other places in which reading groups, usually the smaller ones, have chosen to meet are coffee shops and restaurants. Some groups combine their monthly reading date with an evening out for dinner at a local restaurant. They commonly reserve a big table at the more secluded back of the restaurant where members can meet. These groups usually get together on a weekday night or a Sunday evening when the restaurant welcomes the business. Those who combine dinner with books usually dine first; then, when the table has been cleared except for the coffee cups, the discussion begins, interrupted only by seconds on the decaf.

Is There a Best Time?

Based on an informal survey of reading groups across the country, the evening is prime time. That's a change. Many groups, even just ten years ago, met in the morning or sometimes in the afternoon, but daytime was definitely the time of choice. This is less the case today, as more women have joined the work force or gone back to school. Now, members meet most commonly after dinner, usually at 7 p.m. or 8 p.m. But there are still reading groups, my Booklovers among them, who meet at noon for a delightful lunchtime, two hours of eating and discussion. My other Booklovers group has always met in the late afternoon for a 4 p.m. teatime meeting, just in time for everyone to get home for dinner.

As for what day of the week, most members seem to prefer midweek, though there are some happy groups who swear that a Sunday evening meeting is the perfect way to cap off the weekend or to get set for the week ahead. It depends on how you look at it.

Food, Glorious Food . . .
or, What to Serve?

Food is second only to the discussion of books in importance. To have it or not. How much, what kind, and served when. These are all good questions to settle at your first meeting. What seems to be generally agreed is that all groups serve something, even if it is kept to a minimalist level of coffee and tea.

The most popular refreshments seem to be crackers and cheese with wine or desserts and coffee and tea. A Portland, Oregon, reading group meets at 7 p.m. for hors d'oeuvres, what they call "finger foods," and wine; Miami's semi-monthly Poetry Group makes a fuss about desserts that are often homemade, ranging from a favorite angel food cake to tropical fruit salad. The poetry, often read aloud, continues nonstop right through the refreshments. They must be doing something right because these poetry lovers are reciting and discussing well into their third decade.

Some reading groups still enjoy serving dinner. However, they all agree that it should be served promptly and eaten while social conversation is going on. Then the dishes should be promptly cleared so the book talk can begin. It's no surprise that dinner is important to a New Orleans group, though alcohol rules had to be changed after meetings got a bit rowdy. Now, wine only is served and that is limited to the mealtime.

For some groups, food has been a problem. Both Oxford, Mississippi's group and New York City's Radcliffe College reading group shared the same dilemma: dinner got in the way of discussion. It lasted too long and took too much energy, with not enough of either left over for good literary talk. Until further notice, dinner has been cancelled; as a result, the discussion has gotten more pungent.

FIRST THOUGHTS ON WHAT TO READ

This, of course, is pivotal to the entire success of your group, and the topic will be discussed at length in our next section. Let us just note here that at your first meeting you will want to exchange views with the other reading group members on the kinds of books with which you want to begin your reading.

Are you interested in reading fiction? The classics? Do you want to single out some of the Big Books that you missed and would now like to catch up on? Maybe you want to focus on new books, ones that you've heard talked about or that may have won an important literary prize. Perhaps you want to explore international fiction, beginning with the Japanese winner of the Nobel Prize in Literature, a writer whom you had never heard of but now are willing to try to read. That's what reading groups can do, allow you to reach out toward some writer whom you don't know, have never read, but are now, in this supportive company, willing to try, whether it's something old or something brand new.

At a first meeting, you don't have to settle exactly where your reading is going to take you. All you have to do is agree upon the general types of books you would like to begin to read. Let your direction evolve from there. Agree upon a book to read for the next time you get together. Your members' tastes and their own verbal contributions at meetings will shape your future reading lists and give them a life of their own. By trial and some error, by having open minds and hearts, you will find the books that you and your group do best with.

THE BOOK'S
THE THING

⁓

When all is said and done, it's not when and where you
meet or the refreshments you serve that will determine your
group's success. It is the books that you choose that determine
whether or not your club moves along at a lively clip, where everyone is motivated to read to the very last page and eager to come
to the next meeting to share what they thought about the book
and to listen to what others have to say.

Choosing the Books
⁓

Successful reading groups decide upon the books they are
going to read in different ways. Some groups have a facilitator or
a leader to conduct the discussions; the members sit back while
the person in charge appears at the first meeting with copies of
reading lists, usually books that he or she knows from experience

work well at stimulating discussions. Most groups of the kind we're talking about don't work that way. Members are usually actively involved in the process of selecting their books. In fact, for most groups, this is not only a significant part of the reading group's reason for being, it is also the most fun.

Many groups decide at their organizational meeting what kinds of books they want to concentrate on for the first few months. Nothing is carved in stone. Your group may spend several months reading Victorian novels, enjoying the wonderful breadth of the 19th century in the novels of Thomas Hardy and George Eliot and Anthony Trollope. Then, someone, possibly inspired by the power plays going on in the churchy Barchester novels, may come up with the idea of taking a literary turn and going the social history route with works by Edith Wharton, then moving up to the present with Tom Wolfe and Dominick Dunne, Louis Auchincloss and Louis Begley. Suddenly, you are off, running, and reading for the next few sessions in a different but delightful direction

Sometimes pairing books helps shed greater light on each of them. Jane Smiley's Pulitzer Prize–winning novel *A Thousand Acres* has been called a modern King Lear story. Why not read the real thing, Shakespeare's *King Lear*, and see if the comparison holds water?

Try the same thing with Shakespeare's *Richard III* and Josephine Tey's masterful *The Daughter of Time*, in which a modern sleuth tries to find out if the Evil King really did kill the little Princes in the tower. Keeping your mind open for books that seem to go together or that make neat comparisons or contrasts can help to make your reading even more exciting.

Many reading groups insist that each member be responsible for bringing to the meeting the title of at least one book that she or he would like the group to read. This is a good idea because it keeps everyone actively involved in the selection process.

Often, at an early meeting, several titles are discussed and a few books are then designated to be read over the next months. What usually happens is that titles are put forward to the group with the person who suggested the book speaking on its behalf. Ideally, there will be a general consensus and a few books will be happily agreed upon and put on the roster. Once in a while, however, you will have a member who dislikes a particular author. One group has a novel way of smoothing over what could be a difficult situation by granting each member one veto a year. That means everyone can say a categorical "No" once and the book will be put aside. When that group was heading toward reading *Vanity Fair*, one member absolutely refused. He said Thackeray was too boring, used his veto, and the author was promptly cast aside. At least for that year.

How to Find Good Books

It's not very difficult. Books that lend themselves to great discussions are everywhere—often in your own memory. If you allow yourself to think back to those books that you never read but always thought you would like to, just add them to the list. Remember, they don't have to be "great" books for your group to enjoy them. Books that have a strong theme, complex characters, interesting relationships, or a clear sense of place all lend themselves to discussion.

Not every book works well for reading groups. Some books just don't lend themselves readily to discussion. A highly plotted book, for instance, without much characterization doesn't leave room for much to be said. It is what it is and there isn't much point in discussing some plot twists and turns unless there are psychological turnings going on within the characters as well.

Sometimes books that everyone agrees are wonderful are good to read but lead to some fairly bland sessions. My own Booklovers group enjoys Edith Wharton's novels so much that each season we always read one of her books. Yet our New York reader, Jerry Patterson, says that his group so adores her that their discussions of her novels are "not all that great."

"Our best discussions are when someone doesn't like the book," says Patterson, a Proust devotee. "When we read *Swann's Way*, one couple said, 'This is all very narrow. It's all about duchesses and a society that no one can care about anymore.' I, of course, tried to point out that the book is much more universal. The discussion was very animated and they actually became Proust converts."

GO BACK TO HIGH SCHOOL

Then, too, there are books that you have already read in high school or college. You probably skimmed through them then and barely remember them now, and they surely deserve better treatment than they got that first go-around. Remember Edith Wharton's *Ethan Frome*? High school students get to read that because it's a slender book suitable for class assignment, but not many teenagers get even a scent of its thwarted sexuality. There are lots of others that got short shrift back then and belong high on your list of suggested titles.

A NEW BOOK AWARENESS

Once you're on the alert for books to read in your group, you'll be surprised how many titles will come your way. Keep a keen ear and a ready eye for conversations about books as well as for what is mentioned in the newspaper. I overheard one man talking to three others in the next booth at the neighborhood coffee shop. He was regaling them with an especially quirky scene from *The Shipping News*. I couldn't resist stopping by his table on my way out to tell him that the novel was the very one our reading group was discussing that week. As publishers know, nothing beats word-of-mouth for relaying information about books.

Check best-seller lists, both hardcover and paperback, which often have, tucked in among the highly commercial books, some good candidates. Also look for the Also Recommended list, which tends to include those books that the editors want to call to readers' attention.

CHECK YOUR LOCAL LIBRARY

At your local library, you can look up the current issue of *Publishers Weekly*, the trade magazine of the publishing industry, which reviews forthcoming titles and provides general information about books and authors. Talk to the librarians. They are great resources for what is new and available. They are, after all, in the book business.

FRIENDLY BOOKSTORES AND BOOK CLUBS

Bookstores all over the country are increasingly aware that the reading group member is an excellent customer. Many bookstores have gone out of their way to provide advice, information, and, in some cases, even conference rooms for reading groups to use for their meetings. Some bookstores also provide a discount on book group purchases.

The Tattered Cover in Denver, Colorado, has become a paradigm of what an enterprising bookstore can do for reading groups. First of all, it has Virginia Valentine, who for the past 11 years has worked with more than 250 groups to provide information about books and authors, and to help clients shape their reading lists. Ms. Valentine, who, as the buyer for backlist fiction and poetry, runs a department with the volume of a medium-sized store, works by appointment with book groups, presenting them with a roster of new books that she thinks are appropriate for reading groups.

When asked what "appropriate" means, Ms. Valentine promptly offered both *The Shipping News* and *All the Pretty Horses* as examples. "They dare to be different," she says, "and if they are a little grim, I always tell my groups that those are the ones that make the best conversation." She has even been known to custom-craft a bibliography for a reading group's special tastes. One group, for instance, requested a list of selected books published between World War I and World War II. "That was interesting," she notes, "but it did take a bit of time."

Some of the large book chains that sprawl across the country still take time to consider book groups. Many of them set aside space for groups to use for meetings as well as alerting them whenever visiting authors come to town. Although a local bookstore may not have the facilities or the staff to be as helpful as the larger stores, most bookstores are eager to assist.

Make yourself known at the bookstore. Introduce yourself as part of a local reading group. Become a regular customer. Let them know that you're interested in what is being published that might be suitable for your group. Ask for suggestions on new books, both in hardcover and in paperback. You can plan your reading well in advance, keeping in mind that what is in hardcover today will be tomorrow's paperback.

Reading group membership in a mail-order book club is also a good idea. A monthly catalog offers descriptions of the books, which are offered at discounted prices. Book clubs come in all varieties of reading tastes; you could consider joining any category—mystery, science fiction, theater, history, romance—depending on your group's interests. Together you would decide which selections to order for your reading discussion.

A FINAL SUGGESTION

Check the last half of this book with its hundreds of suggested titles. The books are sorted into almost 40 categories—from "Southern Writers" to "Native American Heritage"—to help you organize your own reading group's agenda. Use these titles as a mainstay for your group's reading and as a way to get started, or to add some variety and flavor to your own lists.

How to Read a Book—
Is There a Trick to It?

∾

Not really. There isn't anything very fancy you have to do in reading a book for discussion that is different from what you would normally do in your own reading. However, there are ways in which a book can be read more effectively. When you know that you are reading a book for the purpose of discussing it with others at a later time, you want to be sure that you have really internalized the significant things about that particular book. When you know the book, when you are familiar with it in the most fundamental way, then you are free to talk about it with real understanding.

Philosopher and educator Mortimer Adler has said that there are three questions to ask about every book as you are reading it:

• What is the author saying?
• What does he/she mean?
• How true is it?

The last question, he says, cannot be answered until the first two have been answered.

If that sounds too much like a Zen master's directive, take another look. All it means is that you must pay careful attention to the central idea of the book. Each author, after all, has something to say and a particular and personal way in which to say it. Of course, it's also true that the better the writer, the clearer the voice. Someone else also said that the better the book, the better the discussion.

ONCE READ, TWICE BLESSED

When you are reading for a book discussion, it is a good idea to read the book twice. The first reading can be swift. It should help you to determine the overall plan of the book, what the main themes are, and how the book is structured. You will get a good notion of the characters, how they interact with one another, and a basic sense of what the author is trying to do.

Then, read the book again. If it is a novel, you are no longer reading to track the plot and anticipate how the book is going to turn out. You can now relate what seemed important to you on the first reading to other aspects of the book.

On this second reading, you can really come to grips with the book. If I own it, I am comfortable with writing my observations in the margins: little jottings to indicate my response to a character, a reminder to myself that here's a nice bit of foreshadowing, or a particularly beautiful piece of prose. This sometimes gets a simple "WOW!"

I also like those little sticky note papers, which are useful to mark pages or paragraphs that you might want to read aloud to the group. I enjoy keeping a notebook with comments on each book that we read. It is especially useful if later you want to make comparisons with other writers or if at some future time you read another book by that same author. It's also a good way to keep track of the books you've read as you are planning what is coming up on your reading group's literary horizons.

HOW
TO HAVE
A GOOD
DISCUSSION

~

*A*ll discussions are good, but some are better than others. If you are already in a reading group, you know what I mean.

After a particular session of your group, you come home elated, invigorated, filled with the excitement of knowing that you have really turned the book inside out. Together with your fellow or sister members, you have truly come to a wonderful understanding of the book, and you did it through a lively exchange of opinions and insights.

That good discussion happens when the group has touched upon all the meaningful aspects of the book. The members have sorted through the more obvious ideas but have also come to satisfying terms with the book's nearly-out-of-reach subtleties. Best of all, they have dealt with the various differences of interpretation with equanimity and respect for others' opinions.

To ensure being an effective, considerate participant in the group discussion, each member would be wise to remember these few simple points. If everyone does, the discussion becomes a "game" in which everyone gets to handle the ball:

Speak up. Group discussion is like a conversation; *everyone* takes part in it. Each speaker hinges his or her comments on what the person before has said. There are no prepared speeches, but rather a spontaneous exchange of ideas and opinions. The discussion is your chance to say what you think. Share your viewpoint.

Listen thoughtfully to others. Try to understand the other person's point of view—see what thinking it rests on. Don't accept ideas that don't seem to have a sound basis. Remember: on almost every question, there are several points of view.

Be brief. Share the discussion with others. Speak for only a few minutes at a time, then pass the ball to someone else. A good discussion keeps *everyone* in the conversation.

Come with questions in mind. As you read and re-read the selection in preparation for discussion, think over the points on which you would like to hear the comments of the group members.

Avoid Literary Anarchy

It doesn't always happen that way. Sometimes one or two insistent voices dominate the meeting and no one else can get a word in edgewise. Other times, a meeting can disintegrate into a free-for-all with half a dozen people clamoring at the same time to express what they think. Or it becomes just almost impossible to attempt to speak a complete sentence because someone else is hard on your heels ready to interrupt. That is not discussion; that is mayhem, otherwise known as literary anarchy.

What to do about it? How do you keep order in a reading group without setting up rules that would ruin the informality most reading groups prize? How do you set up a situation in which books can be discussed with the maximum benefit for all the members?

The New York Public Library, whose dozens of reading groups meet in the various branches from Staten Island to the Bronx to Manhattan, follows the guidelines for book discussions set up by the Great Books Foundation. This distinguished non-profit educational institution was put into motion shortly after World War II by Robert Maynard Hutchins, then the president of the University of Chicago. All NYPL book discussion leaders have taken training based on the Great Books model. For more than forty years NYPL's training was led by Alice Leon, a layperson, who had taken the Great Books training program, which is available to all interested persons nationwide. Although the Great Books has its own methodology for discussions, knowing its system would certainly be helpful for anyone who wants to participate more fully in his or her group.

The Great Books program, for instance, requires two persons to act as co-leaders to facilitate discussion. One actually moves discussion along without ever giving his or her own opinion, while the other person keeps an eye out to be certain that everyone is included in the discussion.

"One of the important things that I learned in working with reading groups is how to keep the discussion going along," says Jan Klucevsek, supervising adult librarian in the Staten Island Borough Office of The New York Public Library. "What is hard is to allow some silence. At first, I kept wanting to fill in with a question about the book. It took me a while to be able to allow a little silence, which gives people a chance to think an idea through and then express themselves. You get some of the more thoughtful observations that way."

A major tenet of the Great Books mode of discussion is that the emphasis is completely and only about the book at hand. The book and the book alone is the thing. No biographical material is allowed to contribute to the discussion. It doesn't matter that Flaubert so adored his mother that after her death, he asked the family housekeeper to dress up on occasion in her Sunday clothes. My own Booklovers group was quite intrigued by that scrap of literary information, which they thought shed some light upon the intensity of Flaubert's characterization of Emma Bovary. Perhaps. But it certainly encouraged us to discuss Flaubert's relationship to women and how it revealed itself in the pages of his masterpiece. It also gave psychological "permission" to touch upon, however briefly in the context of the entire discussion of a complex novel, something of the relationship between mothers and sons as it had been experienced by some of the women in the group.

Another thing that is not in the canon of the Great Books is the use of outside materials to bolster a point of view. No one is encouraged to add to the group discussion by noting that "The critic Alfred Kazin once wrote . . ." or "It says right here in this book review. . . ." Members should not try to persuade or convince other members by quoting the experts. Neither the Great Books nor the NYPL reading groups care what exterior sources have to say. By focusing intently upon the book itself, this mode of discussion encourages the members to think for themselves and to formulate their own opinions based upon their reading. Ultimately, this acts as a very inclusive method, welcoming everyone as equals, whatever their educational background. All that members are urged to do is to read the book with care and discuss what is right there within its pages.

In its training, the Great Books program urges its co-leaders to ensure that every member of the group has an opportunity to express his or her ideas. In order to do this, co-leaders are trained to do the following:

• Ask questions that initiate, sustain, and try to conclude investigations into problems or issues found in the book.

• Ask questions that challenge all unclear, factually incorrect, or contradictory statements.

• Classify all responses according to your best judgment. Select those statements you want to question immediately; ignore those you find uninteresting, trivial, or irrelevant; and table those you may want to question later.

Not every group, of course, has two leaders. In reality, though some groups pride themselves as being leaderless, there is usually a host or chairperson of the particular meeting who is in charge of seeing that the book under consideration gets a full, rounded discussion.

Before You Start Talking

～

Whatever the leadership situation, each member should assume responsibility for the success of the discussions, which means that kind of interplay of ideas that allows everyone to join the club:

Read carefully. That's how you can formulate good, solid questions.

Take notes on the book and mark down any ideas that seem especially interesting. Note difficult words or unclear passages, and jot down the sections that seem to you likely to cause differences of opinion.

Ask basic questions that are directly related to the central ideas of the book. Those are the ones that will encourage the greatest discussion.

Keep your questions brief and to the point. Long, rambling questions will probably lead to answers that are just as unwieldy.

Try to develop the discussion in some depth. After your first substantive question, follow up with another related question so that you are going deeper, rather than more broadly, into the book. Sometimes this means that you will ask the same question, or a paraphrase of it, of different members of the group. Gear your questions to the specific book, rather than asking questions so general in nature that they could apply to other books as well. This will help focus the group's attention on the particular book.

Get everyone involved. Whoever is starting the discussion should refer to each person by name when calling on them. It is usually easier to get things going by asking the first question of someone who you know has a lot to say. Be sure to direct some questions, after the discussion has gotten under way, to the quieter members. Select a question that is interpretive and that just about anyone would feel comfortable taking on.

Secrets of Group Dynamics

Every group has its own selfhood, what we might as well call its spirit or its very soul. This varies from group to group, depending upon the interaction of its members. It doesn't take long for a group to get a sense of itself, for it to feel the bonding that does take place.

It also doesn't take much to shift the equanimity of a group. Think back on any group to which you have belonged, from Girl Scouts to a church choir or a fraternity or sorority. You are going along just fine, until someone comes into the group and everything changes.

A reading group is like any other group, maybe even more so. It is as if a pebble is tossed into a still pool and suddenly the water is ruffled, as circle follows ever-widening circle, marking the smooth surface of the water. A reading group is a very sensitive interrelationship of people who are bound together by something as seemingly tenuous as their affection for books.

That's why, when a group is either starting out or already in progress, it is a good idea to take care when admitting new people. Some groups very much enjoy the renewed vigor and activity that inviting new members brings along. But a word of caution: when you are inviting new members to join your group, try to find out at the outset if you really agree with the kind of reading they want to do.

We heard about one group that had both men and women members. They decided to expand and took in two or three new people. After the enlarged group met for a few sessions, the new members determined that they did not want to read fiction. The discussions that followed became very rancorous, and to some longtime members' amazement, the group could not resolve the issue. They finally decided to disband. The good news is that a core group of the original members picked themselves up and started again. This time they were a good deal more cautious in finding out in advance from incoming members what kind of reading goals they had in mind.

Some groups have kept the same members for many years, decades in fact. They prefer it that way. It's a trade-off. In exchange for familiar faces, the certain sameness of input from the same people, they are able to enjoy the special dynamics created by a group of old friends. For many groups whose members have known one another for many years, the activity of shared reading is one more way of extending lifelong relationships.

It takes a long time to get into that old-shoe mode of reading group. In the meantime, younger groups have their hands full with personalities who crop up in any kind of group situation. What matters most here is that sociability is an important component of a successful reading group. People who read books together like to share warm feelings for one another. Reading groups may welcome disputation about the book to keep things lively, but no one really welcomes the antisocial literary member.

BOOK HOGS, SHY TILLIES, AND OTHER SPECIMENS

Reading is essentially a solitary activity. Reading groups try to make it more of a team sport. It isn't always that easy to get everybody to pull together, but when they do, it makes for a happy book group. Almost everyone who frequents a reading group is great. Members are usually friendly creatures who enjoy books and the people who read them. There are, however, a few odd, if familiar, types whom you may encounter.

The Book Hog. He or she, and this character is surely not gender-specific, likes to talk. This person is not especially sensitive to anyone else in the group. He/she is always the first in and last out of the discussion. Feverishly eager to let everyone else know exactly how much she/he loved/hated the book; if left unchecked, would also include a complete story rundown as well as subplots, just as if no one else knows what the book is about. Fortunately, one of the characteristics of the Book Hog is a porcine hide, so it isn't all that difficult to call a halt by saying some variation of "Wait a minute. Love what you have to say, but let's hear from Jack, or Jane, or anyone else."

Shy Tillie. She is the one who sits at the farthest reaches of the room and certainly doesn't hurt a flea or do much of anything else for that matter. She certainly does not talk or participate in any way. She just takes up a seat that a more contributing member could enjoy. Sad to say, she is customarily female. No one has yet reported a silent male in any reading group. If he exists, guard him well, because there is definitely a rara avis there.

Given a little encouragement, Shy Tillies can thrive in the reading group environment. Those persons who are fearful of being judged and afraid of being found wanting can end up feeling reassured by an amiable atmosphere. A sensitive host or leader can help to bring forth someone like this by directing a question of general interpretation—once a good discussion is already under way—to a member who usually hangs back. What does happen in book groups is that quiet people who begin to feel safe and comfortable make solid contributions to the group.

The Book Group Bull. This one can't wait a minute to share his or her thoughts; as soon as the gate is opened, the Book Group Bull charges forward, snorting and pawing the ground with an important, very important insight. Impatient, overly eager, has to share right now or else this thought might be lost. Steps on everyone else's lines. No point in being subtle, because when the Book Group Bull is in full interruptus mode, no one can get a word in edgewise and disorder prevails. Just say it, straight out: "Stop." "Whoa" also works. Go on and explain briefly that everyone has to be able to finish their thought without fear of someone breathing down their neck or, worse yet, stepping on their lines. Book groups work best when no one feels rushed, when no one person dominates.

Romeo and Juliet. These two romantics, separately, are lookin' for love and reading groups may not be all the wrong places. This is a phenomenon that I admit I have not seen at firsthand, because my own Booklovers have all-women constituencies. I have been told, however, by those who have been there, that reading groups are considered first-rate hunting grounds for men and women who choose to do their bonding with someone of the opposite sex. There is no problem with anyone looking for a mate in a book group, which certainly beats the bar scene. However, the complaint from book groups that have been "visited" by members whose eyes swivel the room for likely future dates is that these people leave the group after a couple of months if no one promising shows up. When one Juliet was called about why she hadn't appeared at the last two meetings, she said it wasn't all that interesting and, anyway, she had joined a ballroom dance group.

The Spider. This is the one who entreats others to follow into a web of private discussion. Not content to participate in what the group may be talking about, Spider weaves an intriguing web in which he or she can reign separate from the mainstream. This is not good, for it saps the energy and distracts attention from the central discussion. Only one discussion should be going on at a time. The leader or host and eventually all other members should indicate right away that no side circuses are to be held, that everyone should pay attention to the discussion in the center ring. The working out of ideas together is what makes a great group discussion.

Tips on Building a Discussion

Good questions inspire, provoke, and encourage participation. Their purpose is twofold: to keep dialogue going and to involve everyone in the group. The right kinds of questions open up the discussion. It doesn't matter if the book is a novel or nonfiction, the idea of expansive questions is the same.

Sometimes, a certain question acts as a key that opens the lock to a freewheeling discussion. Harriet Gottfried, an experienced librarian at The New York Public Library's Hudson Park branch who has trained both staff and volunteers to lead reading groups, recommends offering questions that are as open-ended as possible, to encourage readers to bring their own ideas into the conversation.

"The right question can keep the ball rolling," she notes, citing two examples of questions that keep everyone in the group alert and involved. "When we read Arthur Miller's *Death of a Salesman*, the question was, 'Is Willy Loman a failure?' That was the only question we had to ask. The discussion just took off on its own, which is what we hope will happen because then the group itself takes over and the discussion goes on among themselves." Another question that has proved to be a real attention-getter refers to Kazuo Ishiguro's *The Remains of the Day*: Is this a love story? This simple query called forth an enthusiastic and very varied response.

The questions that open up conversation should be specific to the book at hand; that is essential to good discussions. Some groups ask their members to bring to the meeting questions they would like to hear discussed. That's a good way to get everyone to participate.

ASKING THOUGHT-PROVOKING QUESTIONS

Remember that The New York Public Library measures a successful book discussion by how *much* the group talks and how *little* the leader talks. The leader's job is to stimulate discussion by asking thought-provoking questions. The group's job is to discuss, examine, and evaluate the author's ideas as they are expressed in the work.

Questions like the following can help your group to have open and animated discussions in which everyone participates.

• What is the book about? Talk about the ideas, not the plot.

• What seem to you to be the important themes?

• Is this a book driven primarily by plot, by an idea, or by its characters?

• Ask about the main characters: What are their distinguishing traits and characteristics? What do you admire or dislike about them?

• Describe the interaction among the major characters. What are the most important relationships in the book?

The Victorian novels, great favorites of reading groups, often feature casts of characters who make small appearances, each of which is a magnificently carved cameo. Just think of Dickens and Trollope and the extraordinary way in which they handle minor characters.

• Who are the important, if secondary characters?

• What makes a minor character memorable?

• Does he or she help to move the story forward? For what other reason might that character be introduced?

Discussion of favorite scenes helps to recreate the book and bring it clearly to the forefront of the group.

• What are the most revealing scenes?

• Do they further the action of the novel?

Every book discussed is not perfect. In fact, some of the best discussions are about the flaws. Try to bring that out in discussion.

• Did the book have problems? What were they?

• If you were the editor, what changes might you have suggested to make an even more effective book?

• Are any of the events depicted relevant to your own life?

This last question is a highly direct question that would not be appropriate for all book clubs. Each reading group gets to know within one degree Fahrenheit the personal identification with which its members feel comfortable. After they have been in existence for a while, many reading groups enjoy asking and answering questions that call forth material from their members' own lives. You will soon get the beat of your own group and know how it will react to this kind of question.

When It's Time to Read Aloud

Reading aloud in a book group is a little touchy. Some members like to read passages that they have marked before coming to the group in order to emphasize a particular point or to show some aspect of the book that seems to cry out for an example of the prose.

That's a good idea and it can be most illuminating. It also has to be done very judiciously. We enjoyed being read aloud to as children because it helped us to slip off to sleep. That is not what we want in a reading group. We want everyone to be wide awake, lively, and eager to participate. That's why reading aloud has to be done with care.

Once every few months, some of the reading groups that are part of the NYPL program vary their selections with some poetry. Members take turns reading verse from Whitman and Housman and Matthew Arnold ("Dover Beach" is a special favorite) to Maya Angelou. On these occasions, people enjoy reading aloud and testing their ability to ring out the poetic lines.

Sometimes reading aloud works very well, as when one member selected a marked passage from Virginia Woolf's *To the Light-house* which exquisitely revealed Mrs. Ramsay's subtle character. In some novels—Willa Cather's *A Lost Lady* comes to mind—reading a few paragraphs can capture the flavor of the entire book.

Recently, my Booklovers group was discussing E. Annie Proulx's 1994 Pulitzer Prize–winning novel *The Shipping News*, which, it later turned out from the various interviews I conducted with book clubs across the country, was a novel that many other reading groups were involved in at the time.

Our reading group was very split in its opinions about the book. A few found that the central character, Quoyle, a down-and-out, badly cuckolded newspaperman, was too unappealing even for an unheroic protagonist, and that the setting, the gray, rain-lashed Newfoundland coast, was too grim, too uncompromising. They found the choppy phrases, some of which were not complete sentences, awkward. They could not see how this novel could have won so many major literary awards.

That was how they felt until we began reading some snippets of the prose aloud:

> Water may be older than light, diamonds crack in hot goat's blood, mountaintops give off cold fire, forests appear in mid-ocean, it may happen that a crab is caught with the shadow of a hand on its back, that the wind be imprisoned in a bit of knotted string. And it may be that love sometimes occurs without pain or misery.

Not everyone ended up loving that book. That wasn't the point. It is never important that everyone agrees on how they feel about the book under discussion. But what did happen, after we read aloud just enough to enjoy together the distinctive rhythm and tone of the book, was that no one left the group that day without feeling that she understood the book better than when she arrived, and everyone was touched by the shared discussion.

What I recall with particular pleasure about that day was that one member of our group, someone who one would have felt had little affinity for the doltish protagonist or his seedy world, spoke up and interpreted with great compassion and understanding what the book was all about. Book groups are filled with occasions when people surprise us with such original insights and revelations.

YOUR
GREATEST
RESOURCE:
THE PUBLIC
LIBRARY

❧

*I*t is no surprise that many libraries have taken a center role in sponsoring reading groups. Their business, after all, is books, and book groups are a highly visible way to encourage people to use, enjoy, and discuss them.

The New York Public Library has long been in the forefront of promoting book discussion groups as a way to get more people to read and to use the library's facilities. Although the official NYPL program for reading groups has been in existence since the 1950s, the Library's involvement actually goes back to the turn of the century.

In the early 1900s, immigrants were sailed past the Statue of Liberty and shuttled through Ellis Island, and many were unloaded onto Manhattan's Lower East Side. They had very few material resources. They worked hard, and had little money and no free time. What they had a lot of was children and a willingness to make a better life for them. They also had an unquenchable desire to be "real Americans," to read the books of this new country in its language.

That was when the public library stepped forward to meet a need. Newly formed "Mother's Groups" grew into an important community resource. Each week, during hours when their children were at school, immigrant women would get together with a librarian who talked with them about books. It was free and it was sociable, and it offered one of the few ways these women could meet other women like themselves. Together, with the group leader, they discussed current books and, as a side benefit, they practiced their English.

Today, The New York Public Library still conducts free book discussion groups for the general public. Now, they are usually led by two people who have gone through a leadership training seminar. For many years, this leadership training program was conducted by Rachel Leon, who, even when she was well into her 90s, still shared her love of literature with others.

The leadership training program that she used for both librarians and volunteers is still in effect. It is based on the model developed by the Chicago-based Great Books Foundation, whose methods were explored in an earlier chapter. Basically, that way of leading people into discussion is called "The Shared Inquiry Method," and is very effective for a public library system that places a premium on high-level equality. This system works well because it calls for no prior knowledge of the books and no supplementary literary aids or props such as book reviews or critical analyses. It allows everyone, regardless of literary background or previous education, to read the designated book and then discuss it as part of the group. Even now, there are those trained by Rachel Leon who still impart that sense of inclusiveness that she fostered, that sense of encouraging anyone who comes into a public library to pull up a chair and enter fully into the discussion.

What You Can Learn at the Library

I've always been a sucker for the public library. Maybe that's because my very first job as a high school student was working after school at the library, a modest stone building, set back behind sprawling elms in Plymouth, Massachusetts, not far from the signpost that proclaimed it America's Home Town.

My job was to return books to their proper place on the shelves, which required on-the-spot learning of the Dewey Decimal system of classification. Even better, I got to put magazines away in a tiny upstairs room stacked with periodicals. I would lose myself, kneeling on the floor, poring over the photographs of tribal life in old *National Geographics*, until one of the librarians would poke her head in and tell me to come back downstairs, that there was a stack of books waiting to be sorted.

The library was such a welcoming place; people would come in, stamping their snowy boots on the mat at the doorway, before taking their seats at the long, dark tables where they would read the Boston newspapers or the *Christian Science Monitor* or maybe just sit and leaf through a book, whiling away an hour or two on a winter afternoon.

I don't remember if there were any reading groups that met at that little library, although, as small as it was, it was the place where Mr. Pyle, my high school history teacher, alternated with the Congregational minister's wife to give book talks. Just as simple as that. They talked about a book that had interested them and that they thought others might enjoy reading. It didn't take too long. As I recall, the book talk began about 4 o'clock and, even with questions afterwards, everyone easily got home before supper.

Libraries are still like that, with variations here and there. Throughout this country, the libraries offer some of the last, great free things. Take a look at the reading lists that your library offers. At The New York Public Library's branches, handbills announce when the reading groups will meet next, so the public can be alerted as to what to read and where and when to show up.

There are also an ample assortment of videotapes, from good old films to more recent public broadcasting television series. Many reading groups take these out of the library and watch them individually to reinforce the reading; on some occasions, groups have met to view together such favorite books-into-film as *Jane Eyre, Wuthering Heights*, and *Great Expectations*.

If you haven't ventured into your library recently, try it. You may be amazed at how much good material for your reading groups is available.

Mixing It Up: The New York Public Library Booklists

~

The titles that The New York Public Library librarians have assembled are rich in adventurousness, particularly in the openness and the variety of reading that is encouraged. Not all of the lists are developed specifically for book discussion groups, but the groups often find them useful. Categories of books range from "Celebrating Women," in honor of Women's History Month, to "Earthwatch," with its suggestions of environmental "Green" books.

What is also striking is the breadth and depth of books that are sensitive to ethnic and minority interests. From African American, to Native American, to Gay-Lesbian, to Latino, the library has been widely inclusive in pointing out what is new and well worth reading. Any group can profit by broadening its own reading horizons and adding to their traditional reading titles that offer fresh access to less familiar intellectual territory.

Although it is helpful when the library arranges its book suggestions by themes—women's interests, African American heritage, Holocaust reading, for instance—The New York Public Library, as well as many other smaller public library systems, puts together a lively potpourri of books for its reading groups.

Your own reading group can look to the libraries for ideas on how to mix and match books. Librarians seem to be very adept at putting together books that don't at first seem compatible.

"We try to offer different types of books to attract a broad range of readers. We also like to suggest books that our readers would not pick up on their own," says Jan Klucevsek, supervising adult librarian in the Staten Island Borough Office of the NYPL. "Our readers didn't know about Zora Neale Hurston's *Their Eyes Were Watching God*. They loved it and thanked us for introducing them to her. We find that people are very open to books that they have never heard of."

Take a glance at a few interesting combinations of books that reading groups in the various branch libraries are reading:

For the monthly meetings on Tuesdays at 2:30 to 4 p.m.: Jane Smiley's *A Thousand Acres*, two short stories: Gabriel Garcia Marquez's "The Handsomest Drowned Man in the World" and Harlan Ellison's "The Man Who Rowed Christopher Columbus Ashore," Peter Taylor's *A Summons to Memphis*, Henry James's *Portrait of a Lady*, Henrik Ibsen's *Four Great Plays*, and Virginia Woolf's *A Room of One's Own*.

Another NYPL book group meets on the first Thursday evening of four successive months; they have read Armistead Maupin's *Tales of the City*, Margaret Atwood's *The Handmaid's Tale*, Anne Tyler's *Breathing Lessons*, and Cristina Garcia's *Dreaming in Cuban*.

Yet another group, which meets on the first Saturday of the month at 2:30 p.m., has its own diverse selections: Louise Erdrich's *Tracks*, Samuel Beckett's *Waiting for Godot*, Albert Camus's *The Plague*, Graham Greene's *The Heart of the Matter*, Edith Wharton's *The Age of Innocence,* and Joseph Conrad's *The Heart of Darkness.*

What the librarians, well schooled in both classic and current literature, provide for their groups is something that the rest of us can learn. They are unafraid of mixing it up, of putting on the menu a variety of choices from short stories to philosophical novels to drama to new fiction. Once in a while, the library groups do what they call "dabbling in poetry," in which poems from an anthology are assigned for discussion. One meeting turned out very successfully when the group got highly involved in Sylvia Plath's darkly provocative poem "Daddy." Poetry, drama, fiction—book groups at the library don't care what the format is, so long as the work has validity.

The Suburban Library: A Reading Group Haven

Many small towns and suburban areas take particular pride in their libraries. They have a strong give-and-take relationship with local schools, churches, synagogues, and community groups. Reading groups get encouragement and members from these co-operating institutions.

Wilton, Connecticut, a town of 16,000 located about 55 miles from New York City, is just that kind of community. A historic town marked with rambling stone walls and open meadows, it takes seriously its library and its function in the community. Discussion groups meet at the library, which shares responsibility jointly with local churches and other groups whose members are alerted in advance about the library's programs so that interested persons can take out the books under discussion.

The programs offered are imaginative, both in concept and in the ways in which seemingly disparate books are grouped together. On wintry Sunday afternoons from 2 to 3:30 p.m., the public was recently offered a series, at no charge, called "Caste, Class, and Culture," in which the books talked about were E. M. Forster's *A Passage to India*, Richard Wright's *Native Son*, Kazuo Ishiguro's *The Remains of the Day*, and Anna Quindlen's *Object Lessons*.

One of the programming challenges that the Wilton Library has faced is to offer titles that will bring men into the reading groups. "We actually did get Wilton men interested in coming by offering Merle Miller's *Plain Speaking*, David McCullough's *Truman*, and Tom Wolfe's *The Bonfire of the Vanities*," says Beth Mason, head of the reference department at the Wilton Library, who works closely with book groups. "They got so interested that they came right off the tennis courts in their warm-up suits, ready for discussion."

Attracting people's attention to books is never an easy task, but it is one that the library is willing to attempt. The Wilton Library attracts readers to its discussion series by presenting books under provocative and thoughtful themes:

AMERICAN LIVES: REFLECTIONS ON OUR VALUES
AND OURSELVES TOGETHER

Jules Tygiel, *Baseball's Great Experiment:
Jackie Robinson and His Legacy*
Joe Klein, *Woody Guthrie: A Life*
Garry Wills, *Reagan's America: Innocents at Home*

AMERICAN DREAMS AND NIGHTMARES
Tom Wolfe, *The Bonfire of the Vanities*
Sue Miller, *The Good Mother*
Bret Easton Ellis, *Less Than Zero*

TEMPESTS AND TEACUPS: THE 19TH-CENTURY NOVEL
Jane Austen, *Pride and Prejudice*
Emily Brontë, *Wuthering Heights*
Charles Dickens, *Great Expectations*
Thomas Hardy, *Tess of the D'Urbervilles*
Henry James, *Daisy Miller*

TELLERS AND TALES: AMERICAN CLASSICS REVISITED
Mark Twain, *The Adventures of Huckleberry Finn*
Henry James, *The Portrait of a Lady*
F. Scott Fitzgerald, *The Great Gatsby*
J. D. Salinger, *The Catcher in the Rye*

SPIRITUAL LANDSCAPES IN AMERICAN FICTION
Robert Penn Warren, *All the King's Men*
John Irving, *A Prayer for Owen Meany*
Isabel Allende, *Eva Luna*

Research Tools at the Ready

Many groups like to broaden their knowledge by sharing background material on the author and the period in which he or she lived. Some groups are content with brief biographical information, readily available in any encyclopedia. Other groups want to place the book and its author in a literary and historical context. All the information is at the ready in most public libraries. All you have to do is go and retrieve it.

First, introduce yourself to the librarian. It has always been my experience that librarians are in that business because they like books and, by and large, enjoy other people who like books. They also like reading groups. Therefore, you start out on friendly terms for what might be a long, continuing relationship.

If the librarian is busy, it will be worth the wait to make the personal connection. Settle down, pick up a book. There are worse places to sit and cool your heels. When she or he is free, let the librarian know that you belong to a book club and that you need information to enhance your reading group discussions.

In some groups, every person is responsible for bringing in background information. Other groups designate a different person to do the footwork for each meeting. If you are "it" for the next meeting, you will want to collect whatever seems interesting in both biography and literary reviews. It can be revealing to find out how a book was received at the time of publication and then to contrast that perception with how the author is now regarded.

Researching material to enhance a reading group discussion should not be an arduous task. This is not doctoral dissertation stuff. No one is getting a grade. It's not even pass-fail. It's always important to keep in mind that we are here because we choose to be, because we like to read and because we like to share what we read with others. It's as simple as that.

Here are a few easily used research tools that are readily accessible in most libraries.

The Book Review Digest   Brief reviews of most current fiction and nonfiction. It is published monthly, except for February and July, and has annual cumulations. It is arranged by author, with a title and subject index at the back.

The Reader's Guide to Periodical Literature   A cumulative author/subject print index to general interest periodicals, including many that contain substantive book reviews and articles about authors.

Contemporary Literary Criticism   A multivolume series with representative excerpts from published criticism of novels, plays, poetry, scripts, and short stories. Blue paperbound cumulative indexes will help you locate the volumes you need. This handy Gale publication is part of a series that also includes *Contemporary Authors, Contemporary Authors New Revision Series,* and *Twentieth Century Literary Criticism.*

Benét's Reader's Encyclopedia, Third Edition   A single-volume encyclopedia that includes poets, playwrights, novelists, belletrists, synopses, historical data, major characters in literature, myths and legends, literary terms, artistic movements, and prize winners.

There are countless other reference books that may be useful in varying degrees to enhance your discussions by providing solid background material:

The Columbia Dictionary of Modern European Literature
The H. W. Wilson Fiction Catalog
The Oxford Companion to American Literature, Charles Hart, ed.
The Oxford Companion to English Literature, Margaret Drabble, ed.

Spiller's History of the United States, vol. 2

Major Characters in American Fiction, Salzman and Wilkinson, eds.

Magazine Index Plus on Infotrac   A CD-ROM index to the most recent three years of more than 430 general interest periodical titles, such as the following, recommended as sources for
substantive book reviews: *The New York Times Book Review, The
New York Review of Books, Time, Newsweek, The Atlantic,* and *The
New Yorker.*

Librarians will show you how to use Infotrac to retrieve ci-
tations for articles and reviews. They will also show you how to
use the microfiche reader/printers. Most libraries now have a
copy machine, which, for a few coins, will allow you to copy
pages, in case you prefer duplicating pages rather than taking
notes the old-fashioned way.

Once you get the knack of using the library's resources, you
will feel as if you've struck gold.

HOW OTHER
READING
GROUPS
DO IT

~

*O*ne of the most remarkable things about reading groups is their similarity. Whether they are in Seattle or in Miami, in Portland or in Hong Kong, in a luxurious Manhattan duplex apartment or at the back of a bookstore, reading groups are astoundingly alike.

Simplicity is the watchword that seems to speak to their strength. Most reading groups agree that the best rule is no rules, or at least as few as possible, just enough to set a few guidelines to determine the time and places of the meetings and a format to allow the selection of books and the discussion.

They are, with a few fanciful exceptions, largely nameless.

They are widely known as "The Book Group" or "My Reading Group." There are rarely dues or fees, and only once in a while does a group have a party or an annual celebration. The idea seems to be to take it easy. Keep it simple.

Most book groups are egalitarian and, so long as you have your library card, don't cost a cent. For those who like to use their reading group as an opportunity to build up a personal library, it costs merely the price of the books. There are those who prefer to hire a facilitator, who organizes the group, suggests and helps to select the books to be read, prepares the background material about the author for each meeting, and generally leads the discussion.

Some book groups are not reading groups in the traditional sense but nonetheless offer interesting variations on the book club idea. These groups may pay attention to only one author at a time, reading him or her—it usually turns out to be a him, such as Proust or Balzac—in great depth. Some of these groups are even more specific, reading only one book by one author. The James Joyce's *Finnegans Wake* group provides a good example of members' getting a grasp on singular literary material. Then there are those reading groups who invite to their meetings speakers who address the book and then draw the group forward into a discussion.

The New York Public Library, for instance, offers a special reading program for its Lenox and Astor Conservators; these donors to the Library are invited to participate in discussions led by noted authors in private homes. These Library members are asked to read the book before they attend the meeting so that they can join in the discussion.

What is noteworthy about these NYPL evenings is the often surprising combination of the author-leader and the book that he or she has chosen to discuss. Wendy Wasserstein and Jane Austen? Gay Talese and Nathaniel Hawthorne? The interesting idea of inviting a well-known person to lead a discussion about a book that he or she has admired can be recreated in your own community. Each town, each city, has its own celebrities and they don't have to be authors. You can invite your own well-known person to chair a book club meeting—an event that would make a lively fund-raising evening for your own public library.

Here are some NYPL Lenox and Astor Conservators Reading Groups, with the authors who led them and the books they chose to discuss:

Jane Austen's *Pride and Prejudice,* led by Wendy Wasserstein
Ernest Hemingway's *The Garden of Eden,* led by Toni Morrison
Guy de Maupassant's *Bel-Ami,* led by Tom Wolfe
Henry James's *The Golden Bowl,* led by Cynthia Ozick
Alexis de Tocqueville's *Democracy in America,* led by Richard Sennett
Wilkie Collins's *The Moonstone,* led by William F. Buckley, Jr.
Gustave Flaubert's *Madame Bovary,* led by Francine du Plessix Gray
Nathaniel Hawthorne's *The Scarlet Letter,* led by Gay Talese
George Eliot's *Middlemarch,* led by Susan Sontag
Emile Zola's *La Bête Humaine,* led by John Guare
William Dean Howells's *A Hazard of New Fortunes,* led by Arthur Schlesinger, Jr.

Other People's Reading

Philanthropist and cultural benefactor, nonagenarian Brooke Russell Astor has belonged to book clubs since she was a 19-year-old bride in Somerset County, New Jersey, where she joined a group to help her to connect to a new community. She wrote not long ago, "The reading group experience has helped to discipline my thinking and, indirectly, my life."

Throughout her many years, she has belonged to various reading groups, the most recent of which reads books under the umbrella of a uniting theme. One year, the theme was Manners and Money and the books the group read included Dickens's *Little Dorrit*, Wharton's *The Custom of the Country*, Trollope's *The Way We Live Now*, and H. G. Wells's *Tono-Bungay*. The Beginnings of Revolution came next, with Flaubert's *A Sentimental Education*, Turgenev's *First Love* and *On the Eve*, Conrad's *Under Western Eyes*, and Henry James's *Princess Casamassima*. This year, Mrs. Astor's group has turned its attention to memoirs and is reading Anthony Trollope's autobiography and Edmund Gosse's *Father and Son*.

Reading groups, as we have said, come in all sizes, read all kinds of books, and are as varied as the parts of the country in which their members live, and yet there is an underlying likeness that binds them together. It should not therefore come as a surprise that Hollywood folk join book groups just like everyone else. One book group, which probably is not that easy to get into, includes such famous men's wives as Jane Eisner and Judy Ovitz, with star reader and talker Barbra Streisand. Books read: Jane Austen's *Pride and Prejudice* and Toni Morrison's *Beloved*.

Listening to Readers from Seattle to Miami
◕

No Two Ever Alike

No two reading groups are exactly alike. They may be similar in what they choose to read but each has its own stamp of individuality. Even though the two groups that Evelyn Rosen, historian and teacher, belongs to are only a few miles apart, both in Philadelphia, one downtown, the other suburban, the groups are very different in tone and style.

The first group was founded more than 20 years ago, though Rosen has been a member for "only" about a dozen years. The members are mostly older, retired women, in their 60s and 70s. Though she is younger by more than a decade, she joined because a dear friend and mentor, now in her 80s, was and still is an active member. This book group was a way to keep that contact very close. "I had discussed books growing up with my own mother and I think this was a way for me to continue that conversation," says Rosen.

Their tone is serious, respectful of one another and of the books they select. What governs their reading selections is a desire to read Good Things. They have read Ibsen and Shakespeare, Adrienne Rich and Amos Oz, Woolf and Ondaatje. They do not suffer the lightweight easily.

You can tell a good deal about a reading group not only by the books it has selected and enjoyed, but also by the ones upon which it has heaped scorn. This group did not care much for Pat

Conroy's *The Prince of Tides* (too commercial) nor for Fannie Flagg's *Fried Green Tomatoes at the Whistle Stop Cafe*, a book that Rosen had recommended because her other group enjoyed it so much ("a lot of fun"). Group One dismissed it out of hand ("too slight").

As for the second group, it is suburban, younger in age though not necessarily in intellectual energy. Ranging in age from late 30s to 50s, they are a lively, freewheeling group of a dozen working women. They have a high degree of proprietorship about their reading group. When someone invited a new person to join the group without first checking with fellow members, the recruit had to be disinvited because the members were not prepared to bring in outsiders. This determination to keep the group "as is" rather than admit new members is more common than one might imagine. I have been told of other examples of reluctance to let in a new member either because, as is usually professed, members did not want the group to get unwieldy or, probably more to the point, because the group had already bonded into a unified whole and they were apprehensive that a new person would change the tenor of the discussion.

This Group Two meets every third Monday, "written in stone," and although these busy women at first made certain that it would be strictly business and no food, that has evolved from nothing to cheese and crackers and now to a simple dinner at 6 p.m. before the book discussion begins in earnest.

They have read widely, from *Alice in Wonderland* to Updike's *The Witches of Eastwick* and Jean Rhys's *Wide Sargasso Sea*. They did not like Stendhal's *The Charterhouse of Parma:* too unplotted. After reading Ford Madox Ford's *The Good Soldier*, they rented and watched the video together; they also read John Guare's *Six Degrees of Separation* and then went into New York for a theater trip.

There's no problem getting a discussion going. Each person comes prepared with three questions about the book, and conversation spins on from there. The tone, reports Rosen, is "hysterical, noisy, a free-for-all." Sometimes two or three conversations are going on at once until someone calls out, "Hey, wait a minute . . ." and it quiets down. Once in a while members say they are having an especially hectic time and want to read something short for the next meeting; they even admit that they haven't finished a book. This would be uncommon in the first group, where the women have more time for reading and the length of the book is less important than the substance.

As for Evelyn Rosen, she says that the two groups beautifully balance each other. "I need them both."

ECLECTICISM IS THEIR HALLMARK

What makes Kenneth Lewis's reading group in New York City work for him is the varied nature of its participants. The founder, a woman who is a chef and a voracious reader, in 1991 invited Lewis, an architect, and his wife, Jennifer, a fashion stylist, to join The Book Club, as they call it. They meet with other friends for dinner and conversation every six weeks.

The group is a heady potpourri. More varied than many, it includes a female Wall Street executive, a rock-and-roll entrepreneur, a couple of housewives, a bartender, a Ph.D. in literature, a professor who is a Deadhead, and assorted professionals. At the end of every session, each member proposes a book to be read for the next meeting, and they all vote upon it. Among the books they have read are *Madame Bovary*, *Dracula*, and *The Shipping News*.

"When we have a book like *Alice in Wonderland*, for instance, we each bring in some research on the background, which makes for lively and informed discussions. Each person brings to the group some of his or her own expertise," notes Lewis. "As an architect, I have good observational skills. When we read a novel, I can recognize the underlying themes and how the structure is built."

If The Book Club sounds more serious than most, it isn't. This group marks their anniversary, which takes place at Halloween, with an annual dinner at which they dress up as characters from the books they have read. Last year, having read Dorothy Allison's *Bastard out of Carolina*, as well as *Alice*, they had a room full of Mad Hatters and White Trash.

FROM CHICAGO TO HONG KONG

Another good thing about reading groups is their portability. They travel well. Once you have belonged to a book group, you know how it works and how, if need be, to get one started in any other place in the world.

When Katherine McCaughan's husband was transferred to Hong Kong, she knew that one of the things she was going to miss most was her book group. Now in her 40s, she had belonged to a group in suburban Chicago since she was in her early 30s and her children were still young.

That group, with 10 to 15 members, met each month at a different person's home on Tuesday evenings, with coffee and dessert accompanying the books. An organizational meeting was held each year in September at which it was decided at which homes the book group would meet and who would be the leader each month, because the hostess and the group leader were not the same person. The leader was usually a person who had a special feeling for the book that was being discussed, and she would then introduce it to the others.

Like most reading groups, this one doesn't have many rules, although members did agree that the book under consideration had to be available in paperback and it had to have been read previously by someone in the group. They determined early on that when an "outsider" recommended it or they chose it based solely on reviews, it was less successful than when one of their own suggested that the group take it on.

Just because everyone loved a book also proved no measure of its success for discussion. *Cold Sassy Tree,* for instance, was widely enjoyed, yet the discussion was flat; Sue Miller's *The Good Mother* was flawed, yet it led to a rousing discussion about raising children. "One of our best meetings was about the Southern novel *Bastard out of Carolina,* in which the decision the girl's mother made tore everyone apart," says McCaughan. "Sometimes, when you read about a life style so different from your own, that's when a good discussion really gets going."

Now that she is in Hong Kong, McCaughan has been in quest of a book group. The first one she attended didn't last because the members were too transient; before anyone had a chance to connect, either she or her husband was transferred away. The second attempt was futile because it was too literary; the leader wrote a lengthy paper that she read aloud to the group. When last heard from, Katherine McCaughan was doing what she knows how to do—start her own reading group.

WHEN HOMOGENEITY WORKS

Though some book clubs strive for diversity among their members, one highly successful group is the Radcliffe College Book Group, whose members are, by and large, much more alike than they are different.

This group, which meets one evening a month in various apartments in Manhattan, are all working professionals, lawyers, doctors, and writers. "Our group is extremely well read and well educated," says Elaine Morris, who founded this alumnae group eight years ago by putting a notice in the college newsletter. "We have a common education and a shared background so we are really able to discuss books, often by comparing them to other literary landmarks."

This book group works well without a leader. Members seem adroit at listening well, then taking part in the discussion. "We are somewhat self-monitored," says Morris. "When someone talks a great deal, someone else says, 'Let's hear from Jane or Mary.' The women in our group as professionals are accustomed to being part of discussion groups. They understand about everyone taking part."

There are few working rules, but one is to read only paperbacks and another is not to read popular fiction. They generally read classic literature, with the recent exception of Ondaatje's *The English Patient*, a novel highly favored by many reading groups. "Our Radcliffe women felt comfortable about taking it on as a group activity because several of our members had already read it and saw that it had enough in it to make it worthwhile to discuss," says Morris. On the other hand, they dismissed novelist Alice Hoffman as too light for their reading tastes; her books are now noted as a yardstick for measuring potential books against.

Poor Hoffman is in good company; she is not the only author to have gotten a bad review. What about Melville and *Moby Dick*? The lengthy volume was assigned to be read over the summer months. "They didn't like it. Even though women brought in wonderful references from Greek tragedy and the Bible, it still didn't help. One woman even asked, 'Why did we study this? It got bad reviews when it was first published. It was only because some Harvard professors later said it was a book of value that anyone paid so much attention to it.'"

The Harvard Club of New York is starting a reading group. It will be interesting to see how they feel about the Great White Whale.

OXFORD, MISSISSIPPI

While most book groups are nameless, referred to only as "my reading group" or "my book club," one Oxford, Mississippi, group has a real and substantive name: Mira Bai.

Lisa Pritchard, one of the group's founding members explained that Mira Bai was an Indian princess who lived from 1498 to 1550, wrote poetry to Krishna, and was keenly aware of social injustices. Her character and what she stood for seemed to strike the right note for the group.

When Pritchard and a friend decided to start a reading group, she was no stranger to books. As an employee of Oxford's Square Books, one of the best-stocked, most prestigious bookstores in the South, she had some clear ideas about the way the group would run. At their start-up meeting, they decided that they would read mostly fiction. They agreed that they would choose books at each monthly meeting by consensus and that they would definitely not emphasize food so that no one would have to feel like a hostess.

Despite that game plan, a year and a half later the book group had become more social and less book-oriented. A schism took place and so did a reevaluation.

"We came up with more formal guidelines and that has worked out real well," says Pritchard. "It is important for everyone to bring a suggestion of what to read to each meeting. That way we don't just rely on a few who then tend to dominate the meetings." The person whose book is under view brings in the background information and helps guide the discussion.

Mira Bai is unlike other groups in that its members are often adventurous in reading books published by small presses and or written by lesser-known writers. Though they have enjoyed such traditional books as *The Age of Innocence,* they have also had memorable discussions about such books as Sister Prejune's *Dead Men Walking,* a book about the death penalty, and Marlen Haushofer's *The Wall,* a book first published in the 1960s, in which an Austrian woman finds her inner strength by having to survive on her own. "I found it and loved it and shared it with the group," said Pritchard. "It is sort of a female Robinson Crusoe story with a lot of wonderful internal stuff. It was a real discovery for all of us."

In restructuring their group, they also became more formal about the schedule. They found out what other groups know, which is that the meeting time has to be consistent each month so that members get in the habit of planning other activities around an already determined book group schedule. Mira Bai now meets on the third Wednesday of the month at 7:30 p.m., a time they stay with even if someone can't make it. They also set up some basic questions to ask themselves before inviting anyone into Mira Bai. Do we have space for another person? Will this person be serious about the group?

"When we have agreed among ourselves to ask someone else to join us, we send them a written note," says Pritchard. "It makes it seem important, that her presence is really wanted. That's the same thing as having respect for the books in our discussion."

POETRY UNDER THE PALMS

If ever you get a sinking feeling about the state of literature, a low-down sense that no one reads anymore, just think about the Alfred Boas Poetry Group in Miami, Florida. For 23 years, this remarkable group of 10 to 15 couples, and their occasional guests, has met every other Thursday, after dinner, hurricanes notwithstanding, to sample homemade desserts from angel food cake to tropical fruit salad. They also talk deeply about poetry.

Over all these years, this poetry group has known how to do it. They arrive at their meetings with their *Norton One* or *Norton Two*, or perhaps *The New Yorker Book of Poetry* in hand. These hefty anthologies are their bibles and chief reference works.

The host, who is the provider of the house, the food, and the topic, may also hand out copies of poems to be discussed. A major task for the host is to produce for the evening a guru or some other knowledgeable person responsible for leading the poetry discussion. That person may be a teacher at a local school or college (founder Alfred Boas taught poetry at the University of

Miami) or simply a very literary person who likes poetry and knows how to get into some of its intricacies. This talented leader, who receives a $50 book certificate for shepherding the flock, will give some background about the poet to be discussed and then lead into a careful analysis of the poems themselves, which is really what this group is interested in.

"We can tell pretty much by this time if the leader is depending on just biographical material to get him through," says Ruth Greenfield, one of Miami's community and cultural leaders, who with her husband, attorney Arnold Greenfield, is a charter member of the Boas Poetry Group. "We know a good one when we hear one. A good one will read the whole poem all the way through and in a good voice that helps to inspire questions."

Most of the poetry they read is from the 20th century. They go back to earlier times only for reference. What do they read and who do they enjoy? "Dylan comes and goes. Wallace Stevens stays with us. We have taken to Elizabeth Bishop and we are trying to like Marianne Moore," says Ms. Greenfield, adding, "We did finally get Adrienne Rich."

The poetry group, by the way, is not for everyone. It is exclusive in that the membership is tight: new places are offered only if someone has passed on or moved away. Each couple pays $100 annually, which helps defray the cost of the gifts to visiting leaders. The group has also held a poetry retreat at Key West.

The members of the Boas Poetry Group have gotten older together during nearly a quarter of a century of meeting two times each month. They once thought that their children would inherit their memberships, but most of them are not interested.

IRISH EVENINGS

There comes a time in some people's lives when they don't want any more hors d'oeuvres. They're tired of trying a little of this, a little of that. They are ready to settle down to the main dish. That is what Marilyn Bender, a former *New York Times* business editor, has done since her retirement.

A small notice posted in the window of the Gotham Book Mart, a famous New York literary bookshop, caught her attention. It announced a meeting of the Finnegans Wake Reading Group. This group had not even so broad a focus as a James Joyce society; this one had narrowed its scope solely to the reading and interpretation of Joyce's last experimental masterwork.

The *Finnegans Wake* group meets once a month, alternately on Wednesdays and Sundays, upstairs, above the bookshop. Membership is $1 per meeting. Each month, the newest person in the room starts the reading.

"The group doesn't make a lot of progress, a page or so, while the next person tries to say what it means," says Bender, who has gotten so far into the Joycean mode that she has traveled to London to attend Joyce seminars. "The book is impenetrable, but it is fascinating. You have to hear it aloud to begin to understand it."

On January 13, the anniversary of James Joyce's death, the Finnegans Wake Book Group holds its annual dinner meeting. "You have to have a Guinness or a Jameson to be in the spirit," says Bender. "It's really a wake, but a jolly one."

AGE'S INFINITE VARIETY

Among the positive values that reading groups offer is the opportunity to meet and exchange ideas with people of different ages. In our fragmented society, in which families are scattered across the country, men and women often grow up without close relationships with people of other generations. Yet knowledge of and familiarity with those who are older or younger lends a richer texture and quality to life.

Wellesley College, which has reading groups in various parts of the country, has an active book group in New York City with a broad diversity in its membership's age: a range of nearly 50 years, from the class of 1944 to the class of 1993.

"Many women who come to our book group are looking for a range in ages. That's true especially of younger women who often do not have the opportunity to know people well who are far from their age," says Patricia Murphy, Class of '61, and an active participant in the Wellesley Book Group. "There is a different perspective that we have at different times in our lives and that makes for some extraordinary exchanges of opinions."

The book group is not only widely varied in age, they also swing on the political spectrum from quite conservative to liberal. The books they have read seem to reflect this divergence, ranging from Thomas Moore's *The Care of the Soul* and Deborah Tannen's *You Just Don't Understand: Women and Men in Conversation* to Michael Ondaatje's *The English Patient* and Banana Yoshimoto's *Kitchen*, a book in the magic realism style that was strongly recommended by the younger women but enjoyed by everyone.

They have also read Isabel Allende's *The House of the Spirits,* which was both loved and loathed for its fanciful prose; Jack

Finney's *Time and Again*, admired for its recreation of 19th-century New York but somewhat dismissed as a novel; and William Manchester's historical inquiry into the Middle Ages, *A World Lit Only by Fire*, which, Murphy recalls, "the members had a terrific time tearing apart in a great discussion."

One unusual book they read was Marie Cardinal's *The Words to Say It*, an English translation of a French book about a woman's emotional disintegration and the therapy needed to restore her. It had been introduced to the group by its senior member, a woman from the Class of '44, who had read the book in its original French and thought that her colleagues would enjoy it, which, indeed, they did.

Certain books lend themselves to reading in a group, either because they are difficult to understand or because the nature of the subject matter is too strong for an individual reader to withstand alone. Such a book is Alice Walker's *Possessing the Secret Joy*, a didactic and dramatic account of clitoridectomy. This would seem at first to be a book that some of the older women might find too graphic, but it turned out to be a book to which everyone reacted strongly. "That book was so powerful and difficult in its emotional impact that we were grateful for the book group support," says Murphy. "That's one we were glad not to have done on our own."

A PARADIGM, A PARADIGM

Jerry Patterson's "Reading Group" is one of the most successful around, if you judge on the basis of its members' sense of commitment, compatibility, good conversation, and great reading. This six-year-old group scores high across the board.

The Manhattan-based group has eight members, four men and four women with an ample 25-year age range, from the 30s to the 60s. Most members work in publishing. They meet once a month on Sunday evening at 7:30 for a simple dinner, usually pasta, salad, and wine. At 8:30, the wine glasses are put away, the dishes are carried into the kitchen, everyone settles back, and the discussion begins.

"I think the main requirement for a book group to work is that everybody has to be committed to it. We are all quite serious about it," says Patterson, a social historian and author of *The Vanderbilts*. "If you miss two meetings, you are dropped. We all put ourselves very much into it. We are a talkative group and have had our problems about everyone talking at once. But we are also disciplined so that when someone is talking over someone else, we stop and try to get on track with just one conversation going."

This group largely reads the classics. Until recently, they had read broadly, not repeating any one author, but now they have read two Conrads, two Dostoevskys, and two Dickenses, including *Bleak House*, which everyone liked, and *A Tale of Two Cities*, which Patterson recommends as one of those surprisingly good books that we all read in high school. After reading their first 50 books, they made a geographic tally that indicated they had read 19 books from England, 10 from the United States, 9 from France, 7 from Russia, 2 from Germany, and one each from Ireland, Italy, and South Africa. As for the favorite periods in which they read, two were especially popular. They had read 19 books from the period 1850–1899 and 19 books written between 1900 and 1950.

This group has strong opinions, and discussions are enthusiastic. Among the books they felt best lent themselves to group conversation were Wharton's *The Age of Innocence,* Turgenev's *Fathers and Sons,* Hardy's *Jude the Obscure* (the discussion was good, but the dissension was greater), Samuel Butler's *The Way of All Flesh,* Maupassant's *Bel-Ami,* Eliot's *Middlemarch,* Zola's *Nana,* and Forster's *Howards End.*

For every book they like, there are those that stir negative feelings or, worse yet, not much discussion at all. Patterson is quick to put in his not-to-bother vote for Malcolm Lowry's *Under the Volcano* ("The discussion lasted only about 20 minutes; after all, what could you say about a bunch of boozers?") and Mary Renault's *The King Must Die* ("Very dated. We practically lynched the person who recommended it").

Each year in November, at the anniversary meeting, the Reading Group has a little contest as a way of reviewing and assessing the books they read during the previous year. They answer such questions as: What was your favorite book that we read this year? Your favorite characters? Who was the greatest writer? And, finally, what was your least favorite book we read? "This year they voted it was Olive Schreiner's *The Story of an African Farm.* I recommended it. I'm still living that one down."

BOOK COUNTRY

Seattle is book country. In fact, the Pacific Northwest has one of the highest per capita rates of book consumption in the nation. That is certainly true of Mercer Island, an affluent suburb in the middle of Lake Washington about four miles from downtown Seattle, which has half a dozen very active book groups. "It rains a lot, which probably accounts for our reading habits," says Charlene Volmer, who, for the past six years, has belonged to a lively reading group of women aged 50-plus.

Their name, the Book Bugs, was more or less chosen for them by their local bookstore, Island Books, which gives a 15 percent discount to members of any registered book group. "We said we wanted to be called Bookworms but they said no, that was taken—'How about Book Bugs?'—and that was it."

In an area with so many avid readers, there are many active bookstores. One of them, the well-established Eliot Bay Book Company, nurtures reading groups. Upstairs, above the store in Seattle, free space is available three evenings a week for book group meetings. There are also people on hand to help a group set up its reading lists, according to the kind of books—women's interests, travel, historical fiction, romance, new writers—the group has decided they want to read.

Most Book Bugs are not from the Northwest. "We came here from other parts of the country bringing our reading habits with us. The book group was a good way for people who like to read to find one another," says Volmer. Like many book groups, this one makes a distinction between the hostess at whose house the meeting takes place and the person who leads the book discussion.

Choosing the books is always the most difficult thing they do. They take care of this at one big meeting in January at which everyone comes in with lists of books. After much discussion and winnowing, they decide what books they will read and who will lead each discussion. Their literary tastes are far-ranging. They like Latin literature and have read Garcia Marquez's *Love in a Time of Cholera* and Fuentes's *The Old Gringo*, while also enjoying such Far Eastern books as Mishima's *Snow Country* and Han Suyin's *The Mountain Is Young.*

"We'll try most anything, from Mary Shelley's *Frankenstein* to Hoeg's *Smilla's Sense of Snow.* You could say that we are pretty adventurous readers."

THE GOOD OLD GALS

When you collect any group of Texans, you have a lot of compressed energy. But what about when you get together a roomful of Texas women journalists and media types to talk about books? You certainly can expect a dynamic exchange of opinions and a reading group that is not exactly like any other.

Christy Hoppe, a political reporter, started a book group when she was transferred to the Austin bureau of the *Dallas Morning News,* leaving behind her former Dallas book club. Together with Molly Ivins, the outspoken, plain-talking columnist for the *Ft. Worth Star-Telegram,* they form the nucleus of an irreverent group that sounds like the Good Old Gals. Molly, who is often traveling on a book tour promoting one of her own books—the most recent is *Nothin' But Good Times Ahead*—always tries to make it back to Austin for their meeting on the first Wednesday of the month.

"One of the big reasons we started the group is that we have a nucleus of old friends who never get to see one another. Years ago, we would have met for a coffee klatsch. Now, our reading group is about as close to that as we get," says Hoppe. "When we get together, we really start talking. We have one definite rule: no matter how much we want to catch up on our lives, we have to spend at least 15 minutes talking about the book."

This Texas book group tries to stay current. These are not women who yearn for the tradition and elegance of Victorian novels. "We didn't want to read the classics back then and if we didn't like them years past, why would we want to read them now?" asks Hoppe.

Instead they read the best of new books, most often fiction. A great favorite was Cormac McCarthy's *All the Pretty Horses.* "We loved that book. He really made you feel the changes that the boy was going through. And those descriptions about the richness of the land!" They also read Harriet Doerr's *Consider This, Senora,* but after McCarthy's prose on the Mexican landscape, it paled in comparison.

Hoppe describes their group as "good-natured." "Whoever screams the loudest gets to pick the book," she says. "But no one really cares if every book is not a winner. Even the ones we haven't much liked, we still feel that we have gleaned something from."

For all the rollicking good times these old friends have over their books, they also ask probing questions. How has the author treated the female characters? What moralistic or ethical decisions crop up in this book? How do they apply to your own family?

One of the books that affected the group deeply was *Battle Cry of Freedom*, about the battle of Gettysburg, covering four days in the characters' lives and the decisions that were made that affected thousands of others.

"We asked, 'Is there any cause for which we would die?' 'Are these different for women and for men?' 'What does war mean and what is bravery?'" says Hoppe. "That's the kind of book that we like because we can really get into the philosophical ideas behind it." Although "the Book Club," as they call it, is less than a year old, they have high hopes for its success. "We all read so many newspapers and magazines that maybe we need the peer pressure to make sure that we continue to read books for enjoyment. What's great is talking to a bunch of bright women about what they think about books."

Her advice on starting a book club: Consider the dynamics of the group and how the personalities will work together. Start out with four people and have everyone invite a friend. Keep it small so people feel comfortable. Have plenty of white wine and don't forget the salsa and chips.

DOWN IN THE VALLEY

Book groups are, by and large, nonpolitical. So is LLLL, a lively book group in California's Napa Valley, even though its initials stand for Liberal Ladies Literary League. "We are relatively liberal women who live in a conservative community," says Lauran Posner, who is actively involved in local cultural and civic activities. The reading group, ranging in age from the 30s to the 60s, represents a wide spectrum of working women from two artists, a paralegal, a hairdresser, a speech therapist, a minister, and two women who have founded an alternative middle school.

The potluck dinner sets the tone for LLLL's meetings, which take place every six weeks at one another's homes. "Nobody plans anything, everyone arrives with a different dish, and somehow it always works out to be a lovely mix of food," said Robilee Frederick, a well-known California painter. This same casual attitude goes into deciding what books they will read. For one recent meeting, they were asked to read Amy Bloom's short stories *Come to Me*, as well as "any selection" by Joyce Carol Oates. Members showed up having read different books from the vast Oates canon, which seemed only to enhance the lively discussion.

They prefer reading books written by women writers—Jane Smiley, Dorothy Allison, Marguerite Duras, Edith Wharton— exploring, among other themes, that of female sexuality. The conversations are freewheeling, the women are articulate, and they enjoy an unstructured way of leaderless participation that works well for them.

Napa Valley is a fertile ground for readers. Several book groups have sprung up within a relatively small area. Local bookstores such as Copperfields, Book Ends, and Main Street in nearby St. Helena, and Book Passages in Marin County, provide a nurturing environment by offering information about books, advice on selections, and even some discounted group purchases.

What are the attractions of this book group for its members? "We get to read books that we have heard about and have put off reading because we are all so busy doing other things. Even more important to me is that our book group offers stimulating conversation with women I feel simpatico with," says Posner. "Women are really able to turn to one another for support.

We breath a sigh of relief to have found a group like this. It's important to all of us."

TALES OF NEW ORLEANS

Lisa Slatten, a lawyer in New Orleans, is another reader who belongs to two book groups. It's not because she doesn't get enough books to read by belonging only to one group, but because, in that very social way fundamental to New Orleans life, she gets to spend time with two different groups of people.

The Bookers, her first group, has gone through hard times. The original group was made up of eight single career women. "We were really pressed for time. One was an actress who was traveling, the rest of us had a lot going on in our lives. What happened was that we discussed the book for half the meeting, and then it degenerated into group therapy. We went through the trials and traumas of each of us," says Slatten. "Our lives got more interesting than what we were reading." Two or three of the members got married and the group disbanded.

It was not until a year later that group members realized how much they missed their reading group. They have now agreed to meet four times a year, to try not to make great intellectual demands on one other, to try to be sure that they read the books, and to work together to build the group again.

In the meantime, Lisa Slatten and her boyfriend have joined a co-ed group that ranges in age from the 30s to the 70s and in high-level professions from law and medicine to radio and university development. "Our people resist a very structured group. We are not trying to get a degree in English literature," says Slatten. "We did read *War and Peace*, which we would never have gotten through unless we read it in the group."

Now, at the suggestion of the author Walker Percy's widow, who lives across Lake Pontchartrain in nearby Slidell, Louisiana, the book group has turned its attention to reading short stories, such as those by John Updike and Alice Munro. They rely upon the anthology *The Best American Short Stories* as their primary resource. "Reading two stories for each session doesn't sound like a lot of reading, but we find that we never run out of things to discuss."

SOUTHERN STYLE

The South has a long tradition of clubs in which members, often women, gather to discuss everything from gardening to books in a pleasant atmosphere in which lunch is as important as the subject of the gathering. "People used to join clubs as a way to stimulate social life," says Elizabeth Glaize Helm, a former mayor of Winchester, Virginia, and an active participant in civic activities. "But now, with so many younger women working, it becomes more difficult for them to find time for clubs that are strictly social."

Her book group, The Book Club, is not a reading group in the traditional sense. It is a club and it is about books, but after that, it takes off in its own direction. The Book Club invites speakers to talk about a particular book—Margaret Thatcher's autobiography, for instance—and offers programs relating to books, but what is unique about it is that each member is responsible for donating a book every six months. The collected books then act as a lending library for members. When a book is donated, the donor takes the occasion to give a brief review of the book with some background about the author.

Winchester, in the heart of the scenic Shenandoah Valley, has seven garden clinics in town. No wonder that once a year, The Book Club, with husbands invited, has a picnic at one of the more splendid settings.

THE LISTENING EARS

A very harmonious and successful senior group, both in terms of the longevity of the group itself and of its individual members, is The Book Group, which meets 10 times a year on Sunday evenings at members' homes, scattered over a 25-mile radius in northern Nassau County on Long Island, New York.

Founded in 1976, The Book Group, as members call it, is made up of five couples who are now mostly semi-retired professionals. "Everyone participates. The host of the evening has the responsibility as moderator. He or she usually has gone to the library and brings back biographical material and perhaps book reviews, although we like to discuss the book first to form our own opinions before we hear what the reviewers had to say," says Milton Lipson, an attorney who joined the group 11 years ago.

Discussion moves around the circle, with each person sharing opinions, emphasizing a point by quoting a passage from the book. "We often ask specific questions, such as 'What did you think of this character?' That encourages people to stick to the topic," says Lipson.

The Book Group reads only fiction, sampling works broadly through many centuries and styles of writing. Among books that have stirred lively discussions are Balzac's *Père Goriot,* Atwood's *Cat's Eye,* Smiley's *A Thousand Acres* ("an animated discussion, but an upsetting book"), Wharton's *The Custom of the Country* ("Later, we went on to read her biography."), and Mahfouz's *Palace Walk* ("We loved it because it introduced us to a society that we didn't know about. Several members went on and finished the entire trilogy.").

If they have any problem in this very compatible group, it is that they have too much to say. Cross-conversations are not allowed; if they do occur, they are nipped in the bud by the host, who reminds the talkative members to wait a moment to share opinions with the whole group.

"I think what makes this book group work so well is that we are very respectful of one another," adds Clara Cazzulino, a long-time member. "And we listen. That's important. Not just the talking, but also the listening."

WOMEN'S WAYS

Some of the most successful reading groups were founded by women who cut their teeth on the women's movement back in the 1970s. Barbara Harris was one of them; her book group, Keep on Truckin', continued for 25 years in suburban Westchester County, north of New York City.

"It was a great group. When we started, as young married women raising our children, we were caught up in the consciousness-raising groups of the times, and in the issues that were important to women," recalls Harris. "That ability to talk about ourselves made it easy to discuss the characters in the books and how they related to our own lives." They read and argued about most of the seminal books of women's interest, from Friedan to Greer.

Keep on Truckin' members liked to group books together under a common theme—Southern fiction, Irish literature—which usually lasted for four books; they delved deep into the works of a specific writer, such as F. Scott Fitzgerald, by reading three or four of that author's works. When a writer whose works they were discussing seemed particularly difficult—Virginia Woolf, James Joyce, Thomas Mann—they invited a speaker, usually a local teacher or professor, to give them guidance. Harris recalls that the group collected a couple of dollars from each member and paid $25 as an honorarium.

Eventually, most of the women went back to work and their children grew up and moved on (her own daughter, Lesley Harris, an attorney in San Francisco, has her own book group; see below), but they still held on to the book group. "We had become very close during those years," says Harris, who ran computers for a large corporation.

When she moved to Manhattan six years ago, what she missed most was her reading group. She promptly circulated a letter in her apartment building, asking if anyone would be interested in joining. Some men as well as women responded. One said that he didn't like to read what others selected. Another one sat through the discussion of *Truman*, gave his well-spoken opinion, and then left. Several who showed up at the first meeting dropped out when they found it was not strictly a best-sellers club; some did not want to continue when they discovered that they had to make a regular commitment to read the assigned book and attend monthly meetings.

But now, five years later, the "new" book club has survived; its eight members balance their reading between classics and contemporary books. They look forward to a special annual meeting in December, which is dedicated to poetry. Each person selects a poet she wants to share, and at the meeting she has an opportunity to tell about the poet's life and to read three or four poems that the group will then discuss.

Like many reading groups, this one has difficulty in selecting what titles to read without taking up valuable discussion time. To simplify the selection process, they now pick three books at one meeting. Some members want to read more nonfiction and biography than Harris, who prefers reading fiction. Harris, experienced at negotiating in reading groups, comments, "We are still working that out."

LIKE MOTHER, LIKE DAUGHTER

When Lesley Harris left New York for San Francisco to attend Hastings Law School, she did what her mother, Barbara Harris, had done when she moved to a new community: she started a reading group. Harris, who had gone to Barnard College, used the college newsletter to attract a core group. That was four years ago, and the group now has eight members. "We like this size. If it gets much bigger there tend to be too many side discussions going on," says Harris.

The book group, which has gone beyond its initial Barnard center, is mixed, with three different generations of women from the early 20s to the 70s, some married with children, some single, one doctor, a couple of lawyers, one Chinese, two African Americans.

"The dynamics of the group are really great," says Harris. "It took a while before the bonding started to happen, but now that it has, it has enriched the group. One of the women went through a divorce, another had a history of child abuse, and when these events occurred in novels that we were reading, we were able to bring our experiences to bear upon them."

The one problem that this San Francisco group has is that its members are so well read that it's hard for them to find books they haven't already read. Serious and ambitious in their tastes, they count among their favorites Mahfouz's *Palace Walk*, Hulme's *The Bone People*, Mukherjee's *Jasmine*, Garcia's *Dreaming in Cuban*, Vargas Llosa's *Aunt Julia and the Scriptwriter*.

The group's most unusual project is still under way: Vikram Seth's 1,500-page novel *A Suitable Boy*. "Someone had heard the author speak, thought he was wonderful and that we should read his book. We are spreading it out over three months, 500 pages at a time," says Harris, adding with a pause, "We'll just have to see how it works out."

THE THIRD GENERATION

Elizabeth Hartzell DeSimone comes from a long line of book club members. Three generations, in fact. Her mother, Kate Fiene, the wife of a physician in Palo Alto, California, joined her book club more than 30 years ago; her grandmother, 91-year-old Elizabeth Baker, moved to the Bay Area of San Francisco from the East Coast a few years ago and promptly joined a book group because, her granddaughter says, "she was always interested in new ideas and younger people."

When DeSimone moved to Portland, Oregon, with her husband and three young children, she knew she wanted to start a book club. "After all, I had a mother who went to her book group every month all during my growing up." The problem was that she didn't know anyone in town. "I started conversations with people I barely knew at the local exercise facility, at the co-operative indoor playground; I even put a notice in the neighborhood newsletter." Gradually, she got a group together and now, four years later, they are well bonded.

DeSimone, who is a part-time editor for the local parenting newspaper, now has a varied group of a dozen women whose ages range from the 20s to the 40s; some work full time, some have children, some do not. "For me, my reading group is a way of giving back to myself something good," she says. "Each of the women is at a different stage in their lives. Being at home with young children can be so isolating. What the book group does is to bring a support that goes beyond intellectual pursuits."

Though DeSimone and her mother have long-distance discussions about the books their groups are reading, she sees real distinctions between her group and the one to which her mother belongs. "Our group seems less democratic. We simply assign someone to choose the next book for us to read. Mom's group talks a lot about what they will read, which for us would take away from our discussion time." The older group also does research before the meeting, and the person in charge comes in with reviews, criticism, and biography. "Our group doesn't have the time. Maybe I would if I had CD-ROM data. We talk about the book in any way that moves us, personal, intellectual, from the point of view of the writer, the editor, or the reader. It is all an open dialogue."

Last year, the book club invited the husbands to join them for a social evening and to discuss Grisham's *The Firm*. "We had already read Deborah Tannen's *You Just Don't Understand* so we were prepared when many of the men fell into the pattern that she talks about. At first some were shy, then they just dominated the discussion. It also turned out that many men found it hard to complete the book before the meeting. Men tend to use their time in very different ways."

DeSimone gives one compelling reason for the pleasure she finds in her book group: "I never forget a book that I have read and discussed with my book group. When I look down my list of the books we have read since 1991, I can remember each of them and I can remember the feeling that I took away from the group at the time. When I read on my own, I find that I lose the feel of what I have read."

They have read books that are diverse in degree of difficulty, from Waller's *The Bridges of Madison County* to Toni Morrison's *Jazz*. They also read Patrick Suskind's intriguing and unique *Perfume*. "I thought it was fabulous," says DeSimone, adding, "My mother loved it too."

DOCTORS' WIVES

More doctors' wives belong to book groups than the wives of any other profession. No survey has been done to support that premise, but it is no surprise to Elaine Raitt of Portola Valley, California, whose husband is a rheumatologist. Her longtime reading group, which was started in 1960, is largely made up of medical wives. "We were all young women with small children, married to residents who worked long hours at the hospital and then disappeared into their practice. We had no one intelligent to talk to," recalls Raitt. "Our book group was a really important support group, a place where we could enjoy good conversation, trade our experiences with our growing families, and at the same time read good books."

Over the years, her book group has met once a month, after dinner, lingering on until nearly 11 o'clock, discussing what has turned out to be an amazing array of books. In fact, this California group's list reads like a survey of the best books of the last half of the 20th century. Along with the classics, which they read steadily, they have also sampled then-current books, such as John Cheever's *Falconer*, Carlos Castaneda's *A Separate Reality*, Heinrich Böll's *The Clown*, Eldridge Cleaver's *Soul on Ice*, and Annie Dillard's *Pilgrim at Tinker's Creek*.

As Elaine Raitt describes it, their format is simple and works: the person who acts as leader for the evening gives a sketch of the author's life and works and asks a leading question to begin the discussion. During the course of the evening, the leader may refocus the discussion, add a thought, or toss out another question. The leader usually refrains from revealing critics' comments until the end of the group's own probing of the book.

After they have discussed the book, dessert and coffee are served while they choose the book for the next month, and decide where to meet and who will lead the discussion. As a general rule, the person who suggests a book will not be the leader for its discussion; that way, no one hesitates to suggest a book.

Over the years, the book group has had a few variations: they have read a number of plays but chose only Archibald

MacLeish's play *J.B.* to read aloud, have had authors N. Scott Momaday and the late Wallace Stegner visit to talk about their work, and each year have invited their husbands to participate in a special meeting, carefully choosing in advance a book such as *The Bonfire of the Vanities* that the men would enjoy.

When Elaine Raitt first joined her book club, her son Merritt, now a cardiologist, was only a baby. Now, his wife, Sue Shattuc Raitt, says, "When we moved to Portland from Seattle, I knew I wanted to join a book group right away to help meet people."

Her group, called simply The Book Group, meets on the last Wednesday evening of the month for wine and finger foods. They have read such contemporary books as *The Remains of the Day*, the Delany sisters' story, *Having Our Say*, and the ubiquitous *The Shipping News*.

The young Ms. Raitt's advice to those who move to a new town: "Do it. Join a group. Everybody has been helpful; Powell's, the local bookstore, has suggested titles and helped us to get started. The women in my group have been very friendly. At last, I am beginning to feel connected."

THE REVIEWERS

One of the traditional, old-time reading groups still around is The Reviewers, founded in the 1920s in Colorado Springs, Colorado. It was established to act as a town-and-gown group, uniting both those who worked at Colorado College and townspeople. That 50–50 balance is what they still try to maintain in the membership.

It is not easy to get into this group. That might not bother you, because the rules are stringent. Meetings are held on the first and third Mondays of the month from October to May. The Reviewers used to meet promptly at 3 p.m. for tea, cookies, and books, but as the membership has gotten older, the time has been moved back to 2 p.m., to accommodate the older women who are reluctant to drive home after dark.

Membership is limited so that meetings can be held in private homes. There are now 21 regular members, 4 honorary "venerable women," who have previously been active members, and 2 guest members, who are invited to come for a year, during which time they give a review of a book. At a business meeting, the current membership decides whether or not to ask the guests to join. Usually, it is pro forma and guests after their year-long trial are asked to come along.

There are restrictions also on the books that are reviewed: they must have been published within the past three years, which furthers the group's objective to become familiar with modern thought as expressed in contemporary literature. And the reviewer has her work cut out for her. She first reads sections of the book aloud, tells about the author, and briefly summarizes published reviews.

"This takes planning. You can't just be dipping into the book here and there. There has to be a thread of ideas that follow through the presentation," says Marianna McJimsey, a member of the education department faculty of Colorado College, who joined The Reviewers in 1969. The reviewer's part takes about an hour, followed by 15 minutes of group discussion. The chairperson is the timekeeper, who is precise about the time allotted and enforces the fairly strict rules about members speaking only one at a time. Among the group's favorite authors are Paul Theroux and Jill Ker Conway.

The $5-a-year dues covers mailing costs and the purchase of a book that, upon the death of a member of The Reviewers, is donated in her memory to the Colorado College Library.

LAST
THOUGHTS

∾

My Booklovers is not the first reading group to which I have been attached. Long ago I belonged to another reading group, as a little girl in those years before parents felt committed to structuring children's summer days. Then, in that small town atmosphere, we spent July days ambling in the woods looking for blueberries, learning to swim at low tide, and reading books. Many books.

We didn't read idly. We read in fact with a real purpose. The local public library sponsored a reading club which had a competition in which the goal, as I recall, was to read more books than anyone else during those weeks of school vacation. Each Saturday morning, my friends and I made our weekly pilgrimage to the library, climbed down the narrow stairs to the children's room, which was in the basement, so that from the open windows we could see the white cosmos, like butterflies, blooming just at eye level.

Like reading groups I have come to know as an adult, we had refreshments, lemonade and clover-shaped butter cookies on a gold-rimmed white china plate. But we didn't get the refreshments right away. We had to wait until we had finished making our oral reports on the books we had read during the preceding week.

I'm not sure how old I was, though a clue must lie in the fact that I read *The Five Little Peppers and How They Grew*, one of a series of books about a family that was rambunctious rather than dysfunctional. Another great favorite was *Maida and Her Little Shop*, in which the heroine, a very rich girl, was an invalid who had to be carried about until someone, perhaps her distant but doting father, installed her in a small business, bringing her into contact with kindly poor people whom she helped. Our reading tastes are formed early; I still enjoy books about the rich, and the inventive ways they spend their time.

As members of the summer reading club, we each had a sheet of construction paper in some bold primary color with a green tree drawn on it. Each time we read a book and told its story to the librarian and our book group, we were rewarded with a bright red apple sticker to glue to the branches. By the end of the summer, the reader with the most apples on the tree was the winner.

All these years later, I have forgotten what the prize was, though I think it was a book. I don't even remember if I ever won the prize. What I do recall is the joy that I had in the reading itself, the sense of accomplishment, and the special pleasure of sharing books with others. Nothing changes all that much. That's still what our reading groups enjoy.

THE BOOK-LISTS

*B*ooks are very personal. When we give a book or recommend one, we are telling a good deal about ourselves, our preferences, the things we like, the kind of people, real or fictional, among whom we enjoy spending our time.

What follows are lists of books that could form the basis for many reading group discussions. They are divided into somewhat arbitrary but handy categories to make it easier to sort through them. From "The Big Russians" to "The New Immigrants," from "The International Scene" to "Native American Heritage," these are books to add spice to your reading banquet.

Many of these books are personal choices. Sometimes I have chosen one book rather than another because I had a strong preference for it; that's what we reading group members get to do. We can choose the books we want to read, and then pass on the pleasure by recommending them to others. If one of your particular favorites is not listed among these titles, it may be because I just don't know it or it was not suggested to me. But you be sure to add it to your group's reading lists.

I haven't read all these books, though I would surely like to do just that, but I have over the years read many of them. It's been a great treat to be able to recommend those books that are special to me, which I have always handed over with pleasure to willing friends. Books like Willa Cather's *A Lost Lady,* George Eliot's *Daniel Deronda,* and Louis Begley's *Wartime Lies* are not flawless, but each has some quality that has delighted me. Some of the books that are most pleasurable are underread and, like shy children, need to be brought forward. Those are the ones we love to pass along to our friends.

Other books that join these lists have been suggested by New York Public Library librarians, friends, colleagues, people whose taste I admire. Many of these books have been favorites of reading groups across the country. What really struck me about the books suggested by other groups is how cosmopolitan our reading tastes are. Readers in Seattle and San Francisco are just as likely to recommend Dorothy Allison's *Bastard out of Carolina* as any reader from the Deep South. Regional tastes don't seem to count for much. A book is a book is a book, and a good one leaps across state and national boundaries to be shared and savored by all.

I hope you will use these books and the categories into which they have been tucked as a starting point. They can be easily mixed-and-matched to suit your group's interest and taste. If, for instance, your reading group has always stayed comfortably close to the Victorian classics, you might take a foray into the exciting new Latino literature or some Asian short stories or any category that seems a little out of your customary range. What will happen is that you will be reminded of that excitement that we all used to feel when, as children, we discovered, brand new, a wonderful story.

Books for Booklovers

꙳

Gathered here are some of the books that my own reading groups have read and enjoyed. In reading the list over, I realize that this was a sophisticated collection of books for a "new" club. When I first began leading the group, which we called Booklovers, I knew only that the members were well read and well educated. I also suspected they would be resistant to reading some well-known writer's most popular book.

In other words, reading *Pride and Prejudice* as an introduction to Jane Austen, or *Silas Marner* as a nod to George Eliot, would surely have been met with an exasperated, "Oh, but we've already read that!" Later, as we got to know one another better, and perhaps because they grew to trust my judgment and taste about the books that we would explore together, I could more easily suggest that what they had already read could be re-read. They came to understand that though reading a book for the first time is a special joy, there is a unique pleasure in re-reading an old favorite.

Jane Austen, *Emma*. What a delightful, bossy, annoying heroine is young Emma Woodhouse, who learns about real love the hard way. Austen at her sprightly best.

Jane Austen, *Persuasion*. This is the great one about the melancholy Anne Eliot, who thought love and marriage had passed her by. Even those readers who resist Austen, and yes, they do exist, were captivated by her great, compassionate last novel.

Charlotte Brontë, *Jane Eyre*. Sure, everyone had read this long ago, but it still ended up being one of the favorite books that we read during the year.

Emily Brontë, *Wuthering Heights*. All the intensity and wonder of Cathy and her demon lover, but sadly, most readers preferred the Olivier-Oberon film. You'll have to make up your own mind about this one.

Anton Chekhov, *The Three Sisters* and *The Cherry Orchard*. The tone is autumnal, the mood nostalgic. Russia's landed gentry regrets the past. We had a good time reading choice scenes aloud.

Kate Chopin, *The Awakening*. A wonderfully evocative novel about extramarital longing in New Orleans, written at the turn of the century and happily rediscovered in the 1960s.

Colette, *Cheri* and *The Last of Cheri*. The classic cool and very French novels about a remarkable older woman and the young man who loves her.

Joseph Conrad, *Victory*. What a story! The alienated hero rescues a woman from an all-female orchestra on a South Sea island; they are tracked by some of the more sinister characters in literature. Believe it or not, this powerful novel is about redemption through love. We should all read more Conrad.

Theodore Dreiser, *Sister Carrie*. A powerhouse of a novel about a country girl and a traveling salesman in turn-of-the-century Chicago. Dreiser's first novel and, many think, his best.

George Eliot, *Daniel Deronda*. Eliot's "Jewish novel," about a man raised as a Christian gentleman, who later discovers his Jewish roots and comes to the aid of a beautiful and arrogant heroine, humbled by her wretched marriage. Overlong, overwritten, yet everyone experienced this as a wonderful "discovery."

George Eliot, *Middlemarch*. Certainly one of the great English novels, the story of the intense and innocent Dorothea looking for a cause big enough to contain her magnificent spirit. Coming to grips with this was one of our reading group's most satisfying experiences.

F. Scott Fitzgerald, *Tender Is the Night*. Those beautiful people, Dick and Nicole Diver, in a famous flawed novel about the rich on the French Riviera in the high-stepping 1920s.

Gustave Flaubert, *Madame Bovary*. Poor Emma, she read one silly romance too many. Our group chewed this one up.

E. M. Forster, *Howards End*. Class war among the Brits, which asks and answers the question, "Who shall inherit England?" Forster's complex characters and provocative themes make him a star for any reading group.

Graham Greene, *The End of the Affair*. A great English storyteller whose passionately romantic tale is interwoven with the darkest notions of Catholic sin and redemption.

Ernest Hemingway, *The Sun Also Rises*. Bulls and bars in Pamplona and Paris with a grab bag of expatriate Americans.

Henry James, *The Portrait of a Lady*. James's novels, with their complex themes and shadowed characters, make sumptuous banquets for reading groups. Our Booklovers loved this one about the magnificent Isabel Archer, who has everything yet manages to marry the wrong European.

James Joyce, *Dubliners*. These remarkable stories of middle-class Irish Catholic life conclude with the evocative "The Dead."

D. H. Lawrence, *Sons and Lovers*. An autobiographical novel in which the coal miner's son wrests himself free from the women who love him.

W. Somerset Maugham, *The Painted Veil.* This novel of adultery in the Far East has one of the most provocative opening pages in literature. You can't put this book down. Maugham, who weaves in and out of literary fashion, remains one of the most remarkable authors of page-turners.

Guy de Maupassant, *A Woman's Life.* His first and most compassionate novel. We all but wept over the splendid Jeanne and her misbegotten life.

Anthony Trollope, *Barchester Towers.* Who gets to be the big boss of this little churchy town is the question in a richly peopled, most amusing novel of clerical ambition.

Ivan Turgenev, *On the Eve.* The aristocratic Elena falls for a Bulgarian revolutionary and finds a cause that awakens her.

Edith Wharton, *The Age of Innocence.* Like *The House of Mirth* and *The Custom of the Country,* Wharton's novels of New York social life are always great reading group favorites. We're looking forward to reading her lesser-known *The Mother's Recompense.*

Edith Wharton, *Summer.* Wharton called this her "hot Ethan." Like *Ethan Frome,* it is set in the Massachusetts Berkshires, but while *Ethan Frome* was a wintry book, here, heroine Charity Royall awakens to her own sexuality.

Good Reading

These are novels that many reading groups have pointed out as books that stimulated lively discussion, in addition to simply being pleasurable books that everyone felt better for having read. Not a bad recommendation.

Louis Begley, *Wartime Lies*. A finely tuned novel of memory in which a woman of great fortitude and imagination and her nephew attempt to evade the Nazis as the doors to freedom close.

Paul Bowles, *The Sheltering Sky*. What happens when an odd trio of Americans travel through North Africa after World War II and get caught in the perilous crunch of someone else's culture.

Pat Conroy, *The Prince of Tides*. A richly textured novel about a Southern family's tortured past.

Robertson Davies, *Fifth Business*. The first of the imaginative Deptford Trilogy tells how a misplaced snowball sets several lives on a mysterious course. Readers caught up with Davies's marvelously original story will want to follow up with *The Manticore* and *The World of Wonders*.

E. L. Doctorow, *Billy Bathgate*. The delinquent young Billy interprets the gangster world of the 1930s, which has its own code of honor.

Harriet Doerr, *Stones for Ibarra*. A touching novel about an American couple who retire to a small Mexican village and what happens when the husband becomes ill. Stirs discussion about longtime marriages and taking chances.

F. Scott Fitzgerald, *The Great Gatsby.* Young Nick Carraway observes the goings-on of his reckless cousin Daisy and the self-created Gatsby. Is it the book we remember?

Alice Hoffman, *Seventh Heaven.* Hoffman turns suburban fiction into magic realism when the glitzy Nora moves onto the block with her two kids and amazing things begin to happen. Has some of the glowing heart of *Edward Scissorhands.*

William Dean Howells, *A Hazard of New Fortunes.* Overshadowed by the contemporaneous Wharton and James, Howells is still worth a good look. This one is about social climbing in New York.

William Kennedy, *Ironweed.* It's not Joyce's Dublin, but it is Kennedy's Albany, New York, with its working-class Irish-Catholics and a strongly grounded sense of time (1938) and place that reading groups enjoy.

Barbara Kingsolver, *Animal Dreams.* A woman goes back to her Arizona past to set her present on the right course.

Barbara Kingsolver, *The Bean Trees.* Her first best-seller—followed by *Animal Dreams* and *Pigs in Heaven*—this one is about a young woman whose whole life changes when she finds a baby while searching for her Native American roots.

Cormac McCarthy, *All the Pretty Horses.* Slow and steady as a long buggy ride. The rhythm and magic are cumulative in this prize-winning novel about a young Texan who does some serious growing up on a long trek into Mexico.

Joseph Heller, *Closing Time.* An older but still crackling Yossarian returns in this long-awaited sequel to the classic World War II satire *Catch-22.*

Herman Melville, *Moby Dick.* The masterwork about the quest for the mythic whale. To be read over the summer. Some groups prefer the shorter pieces, such as "Bartleby the Scrivener" and "Benito Cereno," or the novella *Billy Budd.*

John O'Hara, *Appointment in Samarra*. His first novel (1934), which made his reputation. He's not much in style these days, but his novels—including the steamy *Butterfield 8, A Rage to Live,* and *Ten North Frederick*—are richly detailed, poignant dramas of how some others live. Well worth another look.

Whitney Otto, *How to Make an American Quilt*. Eight women gather to sew, talk, and unfold their wonderful ordinary lives.

E. Annie Proulx, *The Shipping News*. This 1994 Pulitzer Prize winner for Fiction is about a burned-out newspaperman, recovering from an adulterous wife, and the children he takes to raise on the stern Newfoundland coast. Stay the course past the beginning chapters, and as the book gathers speed and depth, you will know that you are reading something special.

Norman Rush, *Mating*. An uncommon love story set in Africa, this first novel got great reviews, which compared the author to Whitman and Twain for the generosity of the prose.

Wallace Stegner, *Angle of Repose*. The depths of marriage are plumbed in this novel about an engineer and his forthright wife in the Southwest.

Wallace Stegner, *Crossing to Safety*. An enormously satisfying novel about two couples, a writer and his wife and their rich friends, and how their lives remain entwined.

Anne Tyler, *Dinner at the Homesick Restaurant*. Wonderful insights

into family life and the pains of reunion. One of this prolific author's better books.

Nathanael West, *The Day of the Locust*. If this is Hollywood, you
don't want it. A bitter view of twisted souls as depicted by
a narrow but original talent.

Nathanael West, *Miss Lonelyhearts*. He writes an advice for the
lovelorn column, and the compassion he feels for suffering
humanity just kills him.

Novels with Strong Themes

Everything counts in a novel: character, setting, atmosphere, and, of course, the plot. But the engine that moves some novels is a strong idea which the author has chosen to explore in fiction. These novels lend themselves very well to reading groups. The discussions are just waiting to take off.

Nadine Gordimer, *Burgher's Daughter.* This Nobel Prize–winner understands the South African heart in the midst of moral dilemma. A young woman comes to terms with her father's death in a political prison.

Jane Hamilton, *A Map of the World.* Novels such as this much-admired one, about real or imagined child abuse, have difficult subjects that are definitely softened by sharing them with other readers.

Jim Harrison, *Dalva.* One woman's emotional journey in search of the son she gave up for adoption.

Barbara Kingsolver, *Pigs in Heaven.* A complicated human drama with no easy solutions about the nature of parenthood. Set among the Arizona Cherokees.

Joyce Carol Oates, *Because It Is Bitter, and Because It Is My Heart.* What a prodigious spirit Oates has and how generously she shares it in her fiction, which always seems to reach just beyond. This novel tells of black-white violence.

William Shakespeare, *King Lear.* Read this along with Smiley's *A Thousand Acres* for a powerhouse reading group session.

Jane Smiley, *Ordinary Love & Good Will.* Two novellas whose uncommon subject matter is sure to generate strong discussion.

Jane Smiley, *A Thousand Acres.* What if King Lear and his daughters had lived in the American heartlands? Here's a novel that stirs discussion about the doling out of both love and money.

For the Hip at Heart

What's Hip? That question can certainly set one to thinking about what's the Cutting Edge and who, after all, is Pushing the Envelope. And yet, some of the hippest writers around, like DeLillo and Shacochis, are best known for their earlier works. So if hip doesn't have to be the most current or even innovative, it does seem to have something to do with a special aura that the writer projects, a quality that seems to indicate knowledge of what's really going on. The insider stuff. One question for readers: Why are the writing hipsters mostly male? Her Royal Hipness Tama Janowitz is a notable exception, but then, she practically invented cool.

Paul Auster, *Mr. Vertigo.* An inventive and original writer tells an exuberant tale about the orphaned and street-smart Walt the Wonder Boy, who spins his jubilant way through a surprisingly upbeat pre-Depression America.

Nicholson Baker, *Vox.* An erotic tour-de-force in which a man and a woman, who have never met, exchange lives over the telephone.

Madison Smartt Bell, *Save Me, Joe Louis.* A chance encounter in a New York park brings together two small-time robbers whose spree takes them on a downward Southern route. Smart writing.

T. Coraghessan Boyle, *The Road to Wellville.* That eminent American, Mr. Kellogg, the inventor of the corn flake, is the protagonist in yet another of Boyle's raucous adventures.

Douglas Coupland, *Generation X: Tales for Accelerated Culture.*

These kids have been labeled hopeless and hapless, a not-so-merry band of friends who comprise the twentysomething generation. This is the book that gave them a name. X marks it.

Don DeLillo, *White Noise.* A chilly view of modern days, told through the eyes of a Hitler Studies professor who teaches what was while an ominous black cloud descends over the town.

Tama Janowitz, *Slaves of New York.* The chilled-out New York downtown scene in which assorted artists—avant-garde, performance, and graffiti—find something in common.

Thom Jones, *The Pugilist at Rest.* Down-and-out types like the post-Vietnam prizefighter, explored with strong writerly insights.

Mark Leyner, *Et Tu, Babe.* A savvy novel whose galaxy includes such pop icons as Connie Chung, Jessica Hahn, Ron Howard, and Justice Clarence Thomas in a '90s stream of consciousness.

Tom Robbins, *Half Asleep in Frog Pajamas.* The author of *Even Cowgirls Get the Blues* has slipped a notch down the hipness shelf, but his books still have their devotees and he still comes up with those great titles.

Bob Shacochis, *Easy in the Islands.* A collection of interrelated stories about islanders consumed by too many parties and too much politics. A National Book Award–winner by the author of *Swimming in the Volcano.*

Dani Shapiro, *Playing with Fire.* A fearless first novel about the relationships among two young women and the stepfather of one of them.

Old Favorites

Here are some often-read books, comfortable as rice pudding, for those times when your reading group needs a little soothing comfort.

Louisa May Alcott, *Little Women.* It would be great fun to revisit this childhood classic in the wisdom of your book group. Is Jo still the favorite?

Daphne Du Maurier, *Rebecca.* Yes, you can go back to Manderlay again. Your readers will have a lively time with this romantic yet most artful novel.

Jack Finney, *Time and Again.* This novel about a time trip back to 19th-century New York has been a great word-of-mouth favorite. It may not lend itself to great discussion because it is so much what it is, but what it is is a remarkable tour-de-force.

Ernest Hemingway, *A Farewell to Arms.* An intensely romantic love story set during the Spanish Civil War. Try not to let the Bergman-Cooper film get in the way.

Ernest Hemingway, *The Sun Also Rises.* Long considered his best novel. Today's readers may wonder what all the fuss was about, but that's something the reading group can discuss.

W. Somerset Maugham, *Cakes and Ale.* Subtitled *The Skeleton in the Cupboard,* this is a lively story about a much-celebrated writer and the two women he married. What a storyteller!

W. Somerset Maugham, *Of Human Bondage.* His autobiographical novel in which an art student becomes a doctor.

Colleen McCullough, *The Thorn Birds.* Her first best-seller, and no wonder. This tale about sacred and profane love in Australia is what our British friends call "a cracking good read."

Margaret Mitchell, *Gone with the Wind.* Perhaps you only saw the movie. Try the book; it is really a big, Southern historical romance.

J.R.R. Tolkien, *The Hobbit.* This remarkable fantasy classic about the wonders of Middle Earth makes an unusual interlude for a traditional reading group discussion.

20th-Century English Novels of Comedy and Manners

The Brits do like a good laugh. Whether it's a belly laugh going back to the 18th-century guffaws of Smollett and Fielding, or a rather more subdued chuckle brought on by the wit of Jane Austen, the English novel has always had two distinct pathways, all leading to great good humor.

E. F. Benson, *Make Way for Lucia*. The first in the series of "Lucia" books (*Lucia in London, Mapp and Lucia*, etc.) about a determined and likable busybody in an English village. Her readers often become true fans.

Joyce Cary, *The Horse's Mouth*. A big, broad novel in which larger-than-life Gulley Jimson paints his way into prison.

Stella Gibbons, *Cold Comfort Farm*. When a gentlewoman tries to shape up her ramshackle country relatives, comedy happens.

Rose Macaulay, *The Towers of Trebizond*. " 'Take my camel, dear,' said my aunt Dot, as she climbed down from this animal on her return from High Mass." Now, that's a proper opening line for an exquisitely zany novel about some English on a quest in Turkey.

Nancy Mitford, *The Blessing*. Delightful, very arch novel about love among the aristocracy. This Mitford sister was the one who put forth U and non-U as a way of defining class.

Barbara Pym, *Excellent Women*. If Joyce Cary is descended from the ribald Fielding comedic line, Pym traces her roots directly to Jane Austen. Here, in one of her more popular books, is the clergyman's daughter who gets involved with the vicar next door.

Evelyn Waugh, *Decline and Fall.* This first of his many satiric novels takes on British sportsmanship and the Oxford code of manners.

The Big Russians

Most of the great 19th-century Russian writers are known by their last names alone. Their books, with the exception of those of Turgenev, who spent much of his life in France, are hefty, running to many hundreds of pages, which makes them less accessible to reading groups, who may need more time than the usual month to take on such an ambitious project. Some groups encompass these big books by meeting in six weeks instead of the customary monthly get-together. Others designate these hefty ones for summer reading. Everyone agrees that for sheer satisfaction of accomplishment, it's definitely worth the effort.

Chekhov, *The Three Sisters, The Cherry Orchard, Uncle Vanya.* These are his most commonly read plays, and, together with the *Collected Stories,* give insight into the Chekhovian world of passing nobility, of men and women who never seem to hear one another's song. Autumnal and quintessentially Russian.

Dostoevsky, *The Brothers Karamazov.* On every level—social, political, ethical—and as a page-turning tale of four very different brothers, this remains a 19th-century masterwork.

Dostoevsky, *The Idiot.* Most modern readers get exasperated with the innocent hero, Prince Myshkin, sort of an upper-class Russian Forrest Gump. The whole is surely worth its long parts.

Tolstoy, *Anna Karenina.* Two great stories—Anna and her adulterous lover Vronsky and their counterpoint, the happily married Levin and Kitty—combine in one of world literature's greatest novels.

Tolstoy, *War and Peace.* His first great novel, in which the extraordinary history of Russia during Napoleon's invasion is the backdrop for an intensely personal story in which the characters search for some meaning in life.

Turgenev, *Fathers and Sons.* Generational conflict in the master's 1861 novel of poetic realism.

Turgenev, *First Love.* Romance awakens in rural Russia. A beauty.

Some British Writers

Most reading groups enjoy the high level of literateness, the beauty of vocabulary, and the diversity of even the minor characters in English novels. The following books are especially pleasing.

Martin Amis, *The Rachel Papers.* What happens when a young and cynical university lad really falls in love.

A. S. Byatt, *Possession.* An ornate brocade of a novel about dual romance in both present-day and 19th-century England. A highly intellectual romance just right for the more ambitious reading groups, who will have great fun deciphering it. The author is Margaret Drabble's sister.

Margaret Drabble, *The Realms of Gold.* One of the best of her highly intelligent novels about unpredictable relationships in a Britain in which the political and social rules are changing.

Ford Madox Ford, *The Good Soldier.* Rarely has the buttoned-up Englishman been as artfully revealed as in this novel of two couples who meet annually at a German spa. Subtitled "A Tale of Passion," it has been noted wryly as "the finest French novel in the English language."

E. M. Forster, *A Passage to India.* Events that transpire in the Marabar Caves concern mysticism, racial prejudice, and sex during the days of British-ruled India.

Graham Greene, *The Heart of the Matter.* One of his African novels, this one is about religious faith shattered by an adulterous love. Greene's novels lend themselves well to reading groups, whose members are sure to line up on both sides of the ethical dilemmas.

Ruth Prawer Jhabvala, *Heat and Dust.* A young woman returns to the scene in India where her step-grandmother broke society's reins by eloping with an Indian Prince. The 1975 Booker Prize winner.

Penelope Lively, *Moon Tiger.* A most intelligent and romantic novel recalling Egypt in World War II. If you don't know Lively's delightful, understated literary charm, this is a good place to start.

Michael Ondaatje, *The English Patient.* An astute reading group will help to figure out the enigmatic ending of this story about an unusual trio marooned in an Italian villa at the end of World War II.

Rosamund Pilcher, *The Shell Seekers.* An English family novel in which a mother makes certain decisions about an heirloom painting. Satisfying.

Barbara Pym, *Quartet in Autumn.* A courtly dance of some elderly folk who come to terms with last things in a Pym-ish, wry manner. As dry as falling leaves.

Jean Rhys, *Wide Sargasso Sea.* Remember Rochester's crazed wife in *Jane Eyre*? Well, here she is as the young heroine in this highly original tour-de-force prequel in a Caribbean setting.

Joanna Trollope, *The Rector's Wife.* What happens when the wife of the rector of a small parish decides that she has had enough. The Victorian novelist Anthony Trollope's descendant hasn't strayed far from the family fold.

Evelyn Waugh, *Brideshead Revisited.* The complicated Marchmain family of British Catholics as recalled by an observer who loved them all. The basis of the popular BBC miniseries.

Fay Weldon, *The Cloning of Joanna May.* A 60-year-old woman discovers three wannabe daughters who all look like her. Could be called a DNA novel if Weldon's imaginative force didn't raise it up.

Virginia Woolf, *To the Lighthouse.* An enigmatic impressionist novel about an English family and especially the power of the luminous Mrs. Ramsay. A difficult novel, but most reading groups will find it a rewarding one.

Some French Writers

༄

The great French novels of the 19th century are highly re-alistic and often gloomy about humankind's possibilities for a happy earthly life. In our own century, philosopher/writers like Gide and Camus enjoyed exploring important moral themes and took as their domain the *roman d'idées,* the novel of ideas, in which characters take second place to intellectual inquiry. These examples from both centuries make good grist for the reading group mill.

Honoré de Balzac, *The Human Comedy.* This multivolume masterpiece comprises realistic, usually pessimistic novels that reflect the social order of 19th-century France. The novels *Père Goriot, Eugénie Grandet,* and *Cousin Bette* are particularly readable examples of this great author's prodigious output.

Albert Camus, *The Stranger.* The French novel of ideas is well represented by this narrative of the unyielding Meursault, who faces his own death.

Colette, *Cheri* and *The Last of Cheri.* Age surely has not withered this flawless prose nor the wisdom behind these tales of an older woman and a beautiful young man.

Gustave Flaubert, *Madame Bovary.* Oh, that Emma! Was her doctor-husband the oaf that she thought he was? A classic that stirs impassioned group discussion.

André Gide, *Lafcadio's Adventures.* Another important novel of ideas. This one explores the "gratuitous act," which in this case happens to be murder.

Guy de Maupassant, *A Woman's Life.* This has to be one of the best "first" novels ever written. The story of Jeanne from the freshness of her Normandy girlhood through her life as a disappointed wife and mother. A small masterpiece.

Marcel Proust, *Swann's Way.* The first of the 16 volumes that make up *Remembrance of Things Past,* which Proust wrote between 1913 and 1927. It is always time remembered, memory triggered by events and objects of the present, with a fabulous gallery of interwoven characters. Try this early volume to see if you want to take the leisurely but fascinating Proustian journey.

Stendhal, *The Red and the Black.* A psychologically realistic portrait of the young Julien Sorel, set against the history of the Bourbon Restoration. Ambitious.

Emile Zola, *Nana.* Rugged naturalism about a prostitute whose heart is not always golden.

Southern Writers

No other American regional writers have marked their domain as clearly as have the Southerners. Their tradition is closely held and cherished among their own. Often these writers began their work at an early age, like Capote and McCullers, who did fine work in their very early 20s. They often seem to share dysfunction, wearing their familial distress like some fine if tattered banner. For all the tragic paths Southern writing often follows, there is also a grand tradition of lilting humor.

Dorothy Allison, *Bastard out of Carolina*. Lots of raw emotion here in a very Southern novel about the complex relationships among a young girl, her mother, and a domineering stepfather. The mother's ultimate decision will stir lively group discussion.

Olive Ann Burns, *Cold Sassy Tree*. An expansive Georgia family chronicle with more stories than most novels, even a Southern one, can hold.

Truman Capote, *Other Voices, Other Rooms*. His first novel, written when he was only 24, still conveys the best sense of New Orleans Gothic in all its shrouded splendor.

William Faulkner, *Sanctuary*. About as violent as Southern novels get, this one has a rape (remember the corncob), a brothel, and a Southern belle gone wild. Faulkner's attempt to write a commercial novel.

Fannie Flagg, *Fried Green Tomatoes at the Whistle Stop Cafe*. You may have seen the film, but the book has its own raw texture and reality.

Carson McCullers, *The Heart Is a Lonely Hunter.* After this, her first novel, about an observant deaf-mute, the Georgia-born author went on to write *The Member of the Wedding.*

Flannery O'Connor, *The Violent Bear It Away.* For this Catholic Southern writer, the themes are moral lapses, guilt, and sometimes redemption.

Anne Rivers Siddons, *Peachtree Road.* A romantic and nostalgic novel with a wonderful sense of place: Georgia in the 1940s.

Peter Taylor, *A Summons to Memphis.* A wonderfully civilized story about a middle-aged son called home when it appears that his aged father is about to take a wife. Taylor, from Tennessee, is a modern Southern treasure.

Eudora Welty, *Collected Stories.* She has written novels (*The Optimist's Daughter* won the 1972 Pulitzer Prize), but it is her stories that best convey the richness and diversity of character and symbol of her native Mississippi.

Jewish American Writers

❧

The Jewish American idiom with its rich wellspring of compassionate humor and wry characterizations finds each year other variations on its human themes.

Saul Bellow, *Seize the Day*. An early and brilliant novella about a son who comes to terms with a difficult father.

Ron Chernow, *The Warburgs*. A fascinating account of the German-Jewish family who as leading bankers and philanthropists became special targets for anti-Semitism. A large-scale biography.

Bernard Malamud, *The Assistant*. A shopkeeper takes a hold-up man on as his helper. Brooklyn-born Malamud's stories, those collected in *The Magic Barrel*, for instance, are rich examples of the Jewish American literary genre.

Cynthia Ozick, *The Shawl*. A searing novella about a woman who sees the unthinkable in her concentration camp experience.

Chaim Potok, *My Name Is Asher Lev*. Like *The Chosen*, a novel in which the religious and secular life conflict but a soaring humanism prevails. A first-rate novelist who, when the important prizes are given out, seems undervalued.

Anne Roiphe, *Lovingkindness*. What happens when a daughter calls from Israel to tell her highly assimilated mother that she has joined an orthodox community? Her mother goes to the unwelcome rescue. A novel with a strong theme sure to light hearty discussion.

Philip Roth, *My Life as a Man*. Since *Portnoy's Complaint* (1969), Roth has persevered along new literary paths in an attempt through his un-heroes to come to terms with human longings.

Isaac Bashevis Singer, *The Spinoza of Market Street.* One of his many short story collections—*Gimpel the Fool* is another fine one—in which amazing and magical things happen in highly realistic settings.

Anzia Yezierska, *The Bread Givers.* This is a discovery: a strong 1925 novel about a young Jewish woman's struggle to free herself from the stifling effects of immigrant life.

African American Writers

～

We've come a long literary mile from the years of the Big Three—Wright, Baldwin, Ellison—each of whom wrote an important book during a decade in which it was needed. Now, exciting changes are going on within the African American literary world, in which every book published does not have to be an important one. The news is that there is a profusion of new novels that are simply examples of good commercial storytelling. Some of those popular novels are included here because they represent what is happening; also included here is a selection of those books that touch on important issues within the African American community.

Maya Angelou, *I Know Why the Caged Bird Sings.* Probably America's best-known poet offers her own lyrical explanation of how she got that way.

James Baldwin, *Go Tell It on the Mountain.* An exuberant autobiographical story of a young boy who reaches out to God. The first novel (1953) in an important literary career.

Julia A. Boyd, *In the Company of My Sisters: Black Women and Self-Esteem.* A pertinent issue for African American discussion.

Connie Briscoe, *Sisters & Lovers.* Three sisters with very different lives in a get-with-it contemporary story about love and ambition set in Washington, D.C.

Bebe Moore Campbell, *Brother and Sisters.* A black woman faces some big-time challenges, personal and professional, in a Los Angeles bank.

Ellis Cose, *Rage of the Privileged Class: Why Are Middle Class Blacks Angry? Why Should America Care?* Some self-examination for the growing African American middle class.

Ralph Ellison, *Invisible Man.* From 1952, a quest for identity, often compared to the philosophical search that Camus pursued in his fiction.

Albert French, *Billy.* An enthusiastically reviewed first novel about the execution of a young black boy for an accidental killing in Mississippi.

Zora Neale Hurston, *Their Eyes Were Watching God.* This classic 1937 novel chronicles a beautiful quadroon's three marriages in the black South. The plain-speak takes a bit of getting used to, but the powerful story is worth it.

Sarah Lawrence-Lightfoot, *I've Known Rivers: Lives of Loss and Liberation.* The lives of six middle-aged African American men and women are explored in what the author, a Harvard professor and MacArthur "genius" award winner, terms "an investigation of the human experience."

Terry McMillan, *Waiting to Exhale.* A big, sexy novel of women and the men they choose to love.

Toni Morrison, *Beloved.* A gripping novel that explores the horrific depths of black slavery, covering the Civil War years and later.

Toni Morrison, *Jazz.* Literary layer upon layer, like so many musical riffs, concerning violence in the Harlem of the 1920s.

Dori Sanders, *Clover.* A lyrical coming-of-age novel.

John Edgar Wideman, *Brothers and Keepers.* A trenchant inquiry in which the author explores why he became a writer while his brother chose a life of crime.

Richard Wright, *Native Son.* His first novel (1940), a powerful tale of murder in Chicago, followed five years later by the autobiographical *Black Boy.*

Native American Heritage

◡

It's exciting to discover a new literature—and reading groups are seizing the opportunity to read the novels, short stories, and histories of Native American writers as they explore their past and reflect upon their emerging present.

Sherman Alexie, *The Lone Ranger and Tonto Fistfight in Heaven.* An energetic and likable collection of short stories about the Native American experience.

Paula Gunn Allen, *Spider Woman's Granddaughters.* A collection of traditional and contemporary tales by Native American women.

Mary Crow Dog, *Lakota Woman.* An intensely personal book about what it means to be a Native American and a free woman.

Mary Crow Dog with Richard Erdoes, *Ohitika Woman.* One woman's struggles against alcoholism.

Michael Dorris, *The Broken Chord.* The award-winning true story of the experience of Dorris and his wife, writer Louise Erdrich, in raising an adopted son who suffers from Fetal Alcohol Syndrome.

Michael Dorris, *Working Men.* Short stories about common folk living with humor and hard work on Native American settlements.

Louise Erdrich, *Love Medicine.* The first in her series of novels about lives in cultural conflict in the world of modern Native America.

Tony Hillerman, *Sacred Clowns.* A top-drawer mystery dealing with tribal life shattered by murder.

Barbara Kingsolver, *Pigs in Heaven.* The best-selling novel about a mother and daughter who come to terms with the daughter's Native American heritage.

Wilma Mankiller, *Mankiller: A Chief and Her People.* This autobiography of Chief Mankiller is also an engrossing history of the Cherokees.

Dennis McAuliffe, Jr., *The Deaths of Sybil Bolton.* A *Washington Post* editor discovers that his Osage grandmother was murdered as part of the killing spree in the 1920s against the oil-rich Osage nation. A gripping story of personal discovery.

N. Scott Momaday, *In the Presence of the Sun.* Stories, poems, and drawings by the Pulitzer Prize–winning author.

David Roberts, *Once They Moved Like the Wind: Cochise, Geronimo and the Apache Wars.* Solid and readable scholarship.

Leslie Marmon Silko, *Ceremony.* A widely praised first novel that integrates traditional Native storytelling into modern fiction. Silko, an author of mixed heritage—part Laguna Pueblo, part Mexican, part white—has been an important influence upon other Native American writers.

Anthony F. C. Wallace, *The Lance and the Shield: The Life and Times of Sitting Bull.* An authoritative biography of the great Sioux chieftain.

Patricia Wiley, ed., *Growing Up Native American.* An anthology of stories and essays concerning the forces that shape Native Americans.

Gay Men
and Lesbians

It's about time that so many good, readable books written by and about homosexuals are being published, many by mainstream publishers. A top-of-the-line sampling follows.

Frank Browning, *The Culture of Desire: Paradox and Perversity in Gay Lives.* Understanding gay culture in the United States.

Martin Duberman, *Stonewall.* The history-making Greenwich Village riots as viewed by six witnesses.

Jewelle Gomez, *Forty-three Septembers.* A black lesbian feminist writes about her own poignant search for identity.

Wayne Koestenbaum, *The Queen's Throat: Opera, Homosexuality and the Mystery of Desire.* A most unusual book about opera and those for whom it is a passion. An extravagant and sophisticated book.

David Leavitt and Mark Mitchell, eds., *The Penguin Book of Gay Short Stories.* An ample collection of writings by both men and women.

Stephan Likosky, ed., *Coming Out: An Anthology of International Gay and Lesbian Writings.* A well-chosen and worldwide literary sampling.

Isabel Miller, *Patience and Sarah.* Two women in the 19th century, separated by family, brought together by the farm they share. A classic novel.

Neil Miller, *Out in the World: Gay and Lesbian Life from Buenos Aires to Bangkok.* Some lively tales with an international view.

Paul Monette, *Becoming a Man: Half a Life Story.* The journey to acceptance of his sexuality. Winner of the 1992 National Book Award.

John Preston, ed., *A Member of the Family: Gay Men Write About Their Families.* Experiences with family members and how they accept or reject their loved ones' sexuality.

Edmund White, *Genet: A Biography.* The right author and subject combine for a powerful study of the outrageous French writer and criminal.

The International Scene

One of the great opportunities that reading groups offer is the chance to reach out across national boundaries to sample great books of other countries and other cultures. Our group is always astounded, however, when members compare different translations of the same book and we realize how tenuous and precious language indeed is. Here are some great ones, gathered from countries large and small, from talents that are immense.

Chinua Achebe, *Things Fall Apart.* The Nigerian novelist/poet's first novel, a classic about the effects of Western rule upon tribal life.

Aharon Appelfeld, *Unto the Soul.* A haunting story with themes of survival and spirituality as enacted by a brother and sister, caretakers of a very special cemetery. By the Russian-born Israeli novelist.

Heinrich Böll, *The Clown.* He, too, condemned the German past but also writes of his despair with the materialism of postwar Germany. A 1972 Nobel Prize winner.

Italo Calvino, *If on a Winter's Night a Traveler.* This brilliant Italian modernist has overlaid several "novels" that piece together a mysterious and original fictional mosaic.

Günter Grass, *The Tin Drum.* The post-World War II novel with its dazzling dark symbolism as Germany confronts its own past.

Keri Hulme, *The Bone People.* A New Zealander's novel of dreams and myth about the Maori. A difficult and elliptical book that many reading clubs have hugely enjoyed.

Franz Kafka, *The Castle.* Symbolic, allegorical, and intensely readable, he writes of modern man's soul-wrenching imprisonment.

Nikos Kazantzakis, *Zorba the Greek.* "I am a mariner of Odysseus with heart of fire but with mind ruthless and clear," he wrote, and in all his work, he explored the power of and the conflict between mind and body.

Milan Kundera, *The Unbearable Lightness of Being.* The Czech novelist's international best-seller mingling politics and sex.

Giuseppe di Lampedusa, *The Leopard.* Our Booklovers group took special delight in this richly conceived historical novel about a larger-than-life Sicilian nobleman and the world, as he knew it, declining about him. A big, elegant book.

Naguib Mahfouz, *Palace of Desire.* Egypt's 1988 Nobel Prize winner writes often of paternalistic family life, here set in the 1920s. The literary gods he worships are French: the realism of Balzac and Flaubert but also the subtle fragrances of Proust.

Thomas Mann, *Buddenbrooks.* The decline of a great German merchant family has all the richness of a well-catered banquet.

Thomas Mann, *The Magic Mountain.* The classic *bildungsroman,* the coming-of-age novel, set in a tuberculosis sanatorium in the Swiss Alps at the edge of World War I. A big one, it is well worth making this your summer reading. You'll feel a great sense of accomplishment.

V. S. Naipaul, *A Bend in the River.* Many reading groups have enjoyed this West Indian novel about African revolutionary politics. Also recommended is *A House for Mr. Biswas,* the master stylist's Caribbean novel about the search for personal identity.

Amos Oz, *To Know a Woman.* One of Israel's foremost novelists explores family themes in which a father and daughter struggle to come to loving terms.

Boris Pasternak, *Doctor Zhivago.* A big, lyrical novel translating revolutionary Russia into human terms of love and desire.

From the Far East

Reading groups have expressed increasing interest in learning more about the literature of the Far East. These books, ranging from revered classics to lively contemporary novels, reveal the changing cultural sensibility.

Kobo Abe, *The Woman in the Dunes*. His most famous work, on the meditative subject of the loneliness and self-imposed alienation of modern man/woman.

Kazuo Ishiguro, *The Remains of the Day*. The Japanese-born author lives in England, the setting for this understated novel about a butler in a pro-Nazi 1930s household. One reading group had a great time responding to the question, "Is this a love story?"

Yukio Mishima, *Spring Snow*. A dark love story in which the aristocracy is poised against the nouveau riche in Tokyo early in this century.

Haruki Murakami, *The Elephant Vanishes*. The author was born in Kyoto (1949), lives in Cambridge, Massachusetts, and writes in Japanese. These short stories are antic, surreal, and wildly original.

Murasaki Shikibu, *The Tale of Genji*. An elaborate chronicle of the royal court. The Prince and the women in his life are at the center of this 11th-century novel, which is generally considered Japan's finest.

Kenzaburo Oe, *A Personal Matter*. A 1964 novel about a man who plans to kill his mentally ill son but undergoes a spiritual change that leads him to acceptance. Oe was the 1994 Nobel Prize winner in Literature.

Endo Shusaku, *The Samurai.* A historical novel about the conflict between the traditional culture of the Western world and that of Japan in the 17th century, by a writer much admired by connoisseurs of contemporary Japanese literature.

Amy Tan, *The Joy Luck Club.* Chinese mothers and daughters in California and the long, tough roots that reach back to the China of the mothers' youth.

Junichiro Tanizaki, *The Makioka Sisters.* A rich and prideful family in Osaka on the brink of World War II, in a story told by one of Japan's greatest modern writers.

Ts'ao Hsueh-ch'in, *The Dream of the Red Chamber.* A classic Chinese novel, written in the 18th century, about a large and noble family.

Banana Yoshimoto, *Kitchen.* Quirky novellas about the "new woman" in a surrealistic mode. A best-seller in her native Japan.

The New Immigrants

❧

An exciting generation of newcomers has arrived on American shores. These literary migrants come less from the middle Europe of past migrations than from Asia and India and Latin America. They bring with them wonderful stories from their own mythic pasts as the theme of cultures in conflict sounds loud and clear.

Julia Alvarez, *How the Garcia Girls Lost Their Accents.* This entrancing story about young Latinos on the bumpy road to assimilation was followed by *In the Time of the Butterflies,* a vibrant political novel about the real-life assassination of the Mirabel sisters by the Dominican dictator.

Anna Castillo, *So Far from God.* A literary godchild of Garcia Marquez and Allende. Chicano magic realism.

Sandra Cisneros, *Woman Hollering Creek.* Short stories by the talented Chicano writer.

Cristina Garcia, *Dreaming in Cuban.* Culture in crisis by a promising new writer.

Oscar Hijuelos, *The Mambo Kings Play Songs of Love.* Exuberant cross-culturalism as Cuban brothers get hot in the music business.

Arturo Islas, *Migrant Souls.* An exploration of Mexican-American life on the U.S. border. Cultures in conflict is the recurrent, well-articulated theme.

Maxine Hong Kingston, *Woman Warrior: Memoirs of a Girlhood Among Ghosts.* A tough-minded recollection of growing up in a Chinese laundry.

Bharati Mukherjee, *Jasmine.* A young Indian woman faces the New World with a mixture of trepidation and courage.

Fay Myenne Ng, *Bone.* A strong first novel about the effects of suicide upon three daughters in San Francisco's Chinatown.

Amy Tan, *The Joy Luck Club.* Mah Jong as the *madeleine* which transports these California women back to the China of their girlhoods.

Ed Vega, *Mendoza's Dreams.* How a Latino makes it big in the American culture. A Puerto Rican writer known for his deft irony and good humor.

Nina Vida, *Goodbye, Saigon.* A young Vietnamese survives with style and pluck the vagaries of life in Southern California.

Magic Realism

&

The film *Like Water for Chocolate* turned countless filmgoers' attention to magic realism. People like it. They seem intrigued by this odd combination of fantasy and clear, cool wisdom. Try a few books with this distinctively Latin American flavor.

Isabel Allende, *The House of the Spirits.* A South American epic of both family and politics in high-styled romantic realism. There's even a woman with green hair.

Laura Esquivel, *Like Water for Chocolate.* The Mexican tour-de-force novel in which love and food are equally delicious.

Cristina Garcia, *Dreaming in Cuban.* A new talent writing about a family caught between two unreconciled cultures.

Gabriel Garcia Marquez, *One Hundred Years of Solitude.* The first of the magic-realistic books that English readers talked about and passed along. A modern classic.

Machado de Assis, *Dom Casmurro.* We know so few South American writers. Here's a great one, a 19th-century Brazilian, often compared to Henry James for his subtle characterizations and to Balzac for his realism. Good background reading for the more fanciful contemporary Latins.

Moacyr Scliar, *The Centaur in the Garden.* Come meet one of South America's lesser-known but most splendid fantasists, a Brazilian doctor whose books take your breath away with their wit, imagination, and sheer humanity.

Mario Vargas Llosa, *Aunt Julia and the Scriptwriter.* Peru's foremost novelist with a comic and profane tale.

The Realists

Many reading groups like their books tucked under an umbrella in which themes or prose style bind them together. These novels are very readable examples of realism, by France's tell-it-like-it-is Zola and some of his literary descendants.

Theodore Dreiser, *An American Tragedy.* Probably his greatest novel, this is the 1925 class-conscious story of misbegotten love and murder between high- and low-born.

Theodore Dreiser, *Sister Carrie.* His first novel (1900) and the first of his many explorations into the life of the "fallen woman." Remarkably vivid and still poignant.

George Gissing, *New Grub Street.* The turn-of-the-century British realist who spent time in jail, married a prostitute, and wrote harsh books out of a thwarted idealism.

Sinclair Lewis, *Main Street.* This gently satiric novel about a doctor's wife in Gopher Prairie introduced Lewis as a distinctively American writer.

Frank Norris, *McTeague.* Influenced by Zola, Norris wrote some of America's first naturalistic novels. Grim but powerful.

Upton Sinclair, *The Jungle.* A muckraking novel in which social consciousness overtakes art.

Emile Zola, *Nana.* In this 1880 novel, Zola's heroine never gets much of a chance to rise above her squalid beginnings. Realism at its grittiest.

Reading in Depth

༄

Some readers enjoy mining the literary field in depth. Perhaps they have already read in survey fashion and now want to concentrate on the works of one particular writer. If that's your style, then select a writer whose work encompasses nothing less than the whole world. Here are a few authors whose works do just that.

Jane Austen: From *Sense and Sensibility* to *Persuasion*, all six of the completed novels.

James Joyce: *Dubliners, A Portrait of the Artist as a Young Man, Ulysses, Finnegans Wake.*

Marcel Proust: *Remembrance of Things Past*. His own title in French translates as "In Search of Lost Time," and you should allow plenty of hours to read this multivolumed work about love and its illusions among the elegant Parisian *beau monde*.

Leo Tolstoy: *War and Peace, Anna Karenina, The Kreutzer Sonata, Resurrection.*

Anthony Trollope: The two well-known series by this extraordinarily prolific Victorian novelist are the Chronicles of Barset and the Parliamentary Novels, but he also wrote other wonderful books, including the delightful *The Eustace Diamonds*. No wonder there is an active Trollope society.

Short Books

~

Once in a while, a reading group just needs a short book. Perhaps they have just come off a very long book, like *War and Peace*, or maybe a book that just feels long, like one by Proust. Or maybe the holidays are coming up and everyone is a little distracted. These books are short in length but long in readability.

Julian Barnes, *Flaubert's Parrot.* An arch, quirky little novel about which of two stuffed birds actually inspired Flaubert. Devotees of *Madame Bovary* will want to read this in the same way that they wouldn't want to miss a pertinent asterisk.

Saul Bellow, *Seize the Day.* An unsentimental but ultimately touching short novel exploring the difficult relationship between father and son.

Willa Cather, *A Lost Lady.* A rich and wonderful portrait of a forgotten Western railroad town and the woman who dominated it, as seen by the young man who always loved her.

Joseph Conrad, *Heart of Darkness.* This is the one about the narrator Marlowe who goes into the jungle in search of a missing white trader. It's also about the dark and hidden heart of man.

George Eliot, *Silas Marner.* Only a writer as magical as Eliot could successfully turn an old miser into a masterful hero.

Thomas Mann, *Death in Venice.* A charged and melancholy story about a mature and thoughtful man whose life is changed by a beautiful boy.

Guy de Maupassant, *A Woman's Life.* How amazing that so brief a novel could completely and beautifully encompass the life of its heroine, as well as the world of French Norman nobility.

Herman Melville, *Billy Budd.* This novella, which inspired the Benjamin Britten opera, considers the true nature of good and evil surrounding the person of an innocent young sailor.

Edith Wharton, *Summer.* One of her rural Berkshire novels. Here Wharton explores aspects of sexuality in a story about a young girl, her guardian, and the visiting artist she has come to love. Reading groups could have a very good time discussing the heroine's final choice.

A Second Look

A reading group gives members a wonderful opportunity to re-read and reevaluate a book. Sometimes we read books too early: books that you read in high school are often better served by another look. You may find that what you thought was an old chestnut is actually pure macadamia.

For me, I recalled *Silas Marner* as a dreary book about an old miser with a sentimental attachment to a small blonde child. Rereading it all those decades later, I was stunned by George Eliot's brilliance. Who else would have dared to make a stingy old man—yes, my recollection about that was correct—the hero? And a hero Silas Marner certainly does become. It is a great book and one of those that, when we read it again as an adult, can be appreciated in fresh and wonderful ways. Here are some that deserve another chance.

Lewis Carroll, *Alice in Wonderland.* Some reading clubs reported that when they read this, someone brought in some biographical background on the author and some of the many psychological analyses, which definitely enhanced and deepened their understanding of a book that is definitely not for children only.

George Eliot, *Silas Marner.* A miser whose life is redeemed by love.

Nathaniel Hawthorne, *The Scarlet Letter.* Sin and soul-saving in old New England.

Herman Melville, *Billy Budd.* Like Steinbeck's *The Red Pony* and *The Pearl*, *Billy Budd* gets assigned to highschoolers largely because it is short enough for young students to attempt in a class assignment. This brief novel is about what happens when good and evil come into conflict. It well deserves a second look.

William Shakespeare, *The Tempest.* If you thought this was a fantasy about dwindling powers, look again and read it as a great multicultural drama.

Mark Twain, *The Adventures of Huckleberry Finn.* Life on the Great River as Huck and his companion, Jim, the runaway slave, wend their way through this classic American picaresque novel.

Biography

Life stories don't necessarily lend themselves to the liveliest reading group discussions. A life is, after all, a life. Still, what a biographer has to say, what new information is brought to bear, is important, and when the subject has lived a many-shaded life, then there's room to talk.

Fawn McKay Brodie, *Jefferson*. A nice adjunct to the more standard Malone biography; this is psychobiography at its fascinating best with special attention to Jefferson's complex private life.

Peter Collier and David Horowitz, *The Rockefellers*. That family in a broad and richly textured biography.

Jill Ker Conway, *The Road from Coorain*. This human story of a girl in Australia who prepares herself to face her future in America was a surprising best-seller. Many book groups read it and applauded.

Annie Dillard, *An American Childhood*. The naturalist/writer— *Pilgrim at Tinker's Creek*—and an unusual woman. Her own telling tale.

John Kerr, *A Most Dangerous Method*. The story of Jung, Freud, and Sabrina Spielrein, who had been Freud's confidante and Jung's patient/lover. For therapy junkies, a fascinating triple tale.

Dumas Malone, *Jefferson and His Time: The Sage of Monticello*. Solid biography by an eminent American historian.

William Manchester, *American Caesar: Douglas MacArthur*. Manchester has all the information and flair that it takes to be a first-class biographer, along with a subject who was an American General whose life reflected his own special times.

Robert K. Massie, *Peter the Great.* The biographer's talents are up to his larger-than-life subject.

Richard Rhodes, *A Hole in the World.* A breathtaking autobiography by the Pulitzer Prize—winning author of *The Making of the Atomic Bomb.* A passive father, a more-than-wicked stepmother, his rescue to a boy's home. He endured. An amazing and ultimately uplifting story.

Jean Sasson, *Princess.* A candid look behind the veiled world of the women of Saudi Arabia. Don't envy their gold and jewels; they provide the only sparkle in the women's repressed lives.

Gore Vidal, *Lincoln.* Vidal's considerable historical knowledge combined with his literary license make this a wonderfully readable biography.

Literary Lives

～

Most reading groups have a soft spot for literary biographies. Even if a group chooses not to use them for group discussion, they can be useful as background material. In fact, though there are many literary lives to suggest, there often don't seem to be enough well-crafted biographies that color the aspects of the person and the artist with equally subtle strokes. Here are some that seem to work extremely well.

Isak Dinesen, *Out of Africa.* The Baroness Blixen's remarkable years on her West African farm.

Margaret Forster, *Daphne Du Maurier: The Secret Life of the Renowned Storyteller.* Britain's beloved mistress of high romance had her own mysteries, well recorded here by one of England's newer novelists.

Arthur and Barbara Gelb, *O'Neill.* The dramatist's life story with all the pain that led directly to all the plays.

Justin Kaplan, *Walt Whitman.* Poet and journalist, this "Bard of democracy" was an original in both his verse and his life.

R.W. B. Lewis, *Edith Wharton.* This award-winning biography covers Wharton's neurasthenic Newport girlhood through her years as a New York society wife to her prolific glory years in Paris.

R.W. B. Lewis, *The Jameses: A Family Narrative.* That remarkable family of achievers and why they seemed to live such anemic personal lives.

Ted Morgan, *Maugham.* A highly readable account of the long and prolific life (1874–1965) of a traveling man who had so many dazzling friends—from Cole Porter to Churchill —that it's amazing he ever wrote at all.

Graham Robb, *Balzac: A Life.* Probably too abundant a book for one reading group session, but this is, after all, the author who could eat 100 oysters at a sitting.

Phyllis Rose, *Parallel Lives.* The marriages of five Victorian writers from Dickens to Eliot and the various and always interesting ways in which they worked.

Jean Strouse, *Alice James: A Biography.* The James brothers' only sister, whose ailing and misbegotten life was spent often abroad in a "Boston marriage," though the author indicates that if given half a chance, she might have outshone the rest of her brilliant family.

Theater

～

Some plays belong strictly in the theater. Others lend themselves to reading aloud, both privately and in a group; some dramatists, like Ibsen and Miller, for instance, will always inspire lively discussions. One reading group member mentioned that when the question "Was Willy Loman a success?" was asked, an excited discussion took off for an hour. These plays are suggested because they seem to have that provocative edge that leads to good conversation.

Selected Plays of Edward Albee. Who's Afraid of Virginia Woolf? The Zoo Story, etc.

Jean Anouilh, *Antigone.*

Clive Barnes, ed., *The Best American Plays 1983–1992.* Ninth Series.

Bertolt Brecht, *Mother Courage and Her Children.*

Brian Friel, *Dancing at Lughnasa.*

A. R. Gurney, *The Old Boy.*

Henrik Ibsen, *A Doll's House.*

Henrik Ibsen, *Hedda Gabler.*

Tony Kushner, *Angels in America,* Parts I and II.

Brooks McNamara, ed., *Plays from the Contemporary British Theater.*

Arthur Miller, *Death of a Salesman.*

Sean O'Casey, *Juno and the Paycock.*

Eugene O'Neill, *Mourning Becomes Electra.*

Eugene O'Neill, *Strange Interlude.*

Luigi Pirandello, *Six Characters in Search of an Author.*

Jean-Paul Sartre, *No Exit.*
August Strindberg, *Miss Julie.*
Wendy Wasserstein, *The Sisters Rosensweig.*
Tennessee Williams, *The Glass Menagerie.*
August Wilson, *The Piano Lesson.*
Lanford Wilson, *Redwood Curtain.*

Short Stories

～

Some reading groups enjoy occasionally sparking their customary booklists with a collection of short stories. It's always interesting to compare the intensity of the short story form with that of longer pieces of fiction. Here are some particularly well-loved writers and their works.

Ann Beattie, *Chilly Scenes of Winter.* A minimalist whose stories of relationships gone awry lead to lively conversation.

Raymond Carver, *Cathedral.* He has been called the Edward Hopper of the short story. Spare, lonely, and as clear as ice.

John Cheever, *The Enormous Radio.* These stories, many of which appeared in *The New Yorker* in the 1950s, still have the power to amaze us with their graceful blend of irony and compassion.

James Joyce, *Dubliners.* Before Joyce went on his self-imposed exile from his native land, he wrote these astoundingly clear stories about the men and women who struggled for breath in the Dublin of confinement. The concluding story, "The Dead," is a Joycean masterwork.

Alice Munro, *Friend of My Youth.* Cynthia Ozick calls Munro "our Chekhov." She's a great favorite with reading groups. Her new collection, *Open Secrets*, focuses upon a small Canadian town where one mystery after another, like life itself, has a way of unfolding.

Tillie Olsen, *Tell Me a Riddle.* Olsen didn't publish until late middle age. Her stories have just that remarkable sense of maturity and wisdom. If you don't know this wise bird's work, seek it out.

Grace Paley, *Little Disturbances of Man.* These small stories tell everything, written by a woman who, in her fiction, is always generous with her Jewish, female, urban self. Newly available is *Collected Stories*.

Katherine Anne Porter, *Pale Horse, Pale Rider.* Three short novels, including *Noon Wine* and *Old Mortality*, typical of her style, in which more is implied than stated. Leads to a good discussion.

Tobias Wolfe, ed., *The Vintage Book of Contemporary American Short Stories.* A lively anthology that is varied in the authors' geography, style, and content but consistent in the high quality of the prose. Among the writers are Richard Ford, Barry Hannah, Jamaica Kincaid, and Dorothy Allison.

Travel Notes

༄

The literary world in which travel writers live has never looked better. There are a host of good writers, some of whom are also novelists, whose observations about the places they have visited and the sights they have seen lend themselves to good discussion among armchair travelers.

Paul Bowles, *Their Heads Are Green and Their Hands Are Blue: Scenes from the Non-Christian World.* The meanderings of the novelist and literary gypsy from Ceylon to Morocco.

Bruce Chatwin, *The Songlines.* The Australian Outback and a search by the mysterious Aboriginal peoples for the meaning of their age-old Dreaming-tracks.

M.F.K. Fisher, *Long Ago in France.* A small, gentle book, and a very touching one, about her early years in Burgundy when the world of food and love was still brand new.

Pico Iyer, *Falling Off the Map: Some Lonely Places of the World.* The author of the irrepressible *Video Night in Kathmandu* is considered a postmodern travel writer, which means that he is often funny and always irreverent.

Mary McCarthy, *The Stones of Florence.* A wonderfully dense and writerly book about that elegant city's art and architecture.

James Michener, *Iberia.* This was clearly a labor of love. The novelist's panoramic view of Spain remains one of his most rewarding and reflective books.

Henry Miller, *The Colossus of Maroussi.* Whatever he wrote, Miller was always intensely personal. This time the country is Greece and the observations are uniquely his own.

Jan Morris, *Locations.* Everything she writes is deeply felt and closely observed. Here are travel pieces about far-flung places from Canberra to Japan to Vermont.

Mary Lee Settle, *Turkish Selections.* When this novelist turns her attention to a distant and wondrous land, she comes up with extraordinary observations.

Paul Theroux, *The Happy Isles of Oceania.* From New Zealand to New Guinea, this peripatetic voyager paddles his way through the Pacific. Also recommended: *Riding the Iron Rooster,* an account of the author's arduous train ride through China.

Some Science Books

୧

Reading groups haven't paid much attention to books relating to the sciences, but reading books of science together could be immensely helpful. Many "popular" science books—Stephen Hawking's *A Brief History of Time* comes to mind as a prime example—require too much diligence and too much previous knowledge for the lay reader to handle them alone. Perhaps in the context of a reading group, where members can discuss the issues, what seems complex could be made clear. Also, many of the new science books bring to the fore provocative questions about the essence of life and its place in the universe that would offer great substance for reading group discussions. Here are a few books to get you started on what could be an exciting road.

Ronald W. Clark, *Einstein: The Life and Times.* What a remarkable life he led and what an uncommon man he was—a spiritual man and a pacifist, whose view of space and time changed the way we think about the universe. This is a straightforward and classic biography.

Freeman Dyson, *Disturbing the Universe.* The intellectual autobiography of a world-renowned theoretical physicist, filled with insights about the essence of science in the 20th century.

Richard Feynman, *Surely You're Joking, Mr. Feynman!* The absorbing autobiography of the Nobel Prize–winning physicist, who was eccentric, brilliant, and, in the circles in which he traveled, legendary. This would pair well with James Gleick's best-selling Feynman biography, *Genius.*

James Gleick, *Chaos: Making a New Science.* This highly popular book about the underpinnings of the universe requires attentive reading. A reading group can surely help plumb its depths.

Stephen Jay Gould, *The Panda's Thumb: More Reflections in Natural History.* This prolific scientist has written several excellent books—a new one is *Eight Little Piggies*—relating our human connection to our historic and biological past.

Carl Sagan, *Cosmos.* An authentic attempt to present theoretical information in accessible, even graceful prose for the layperson who wants to understand such imponderables as Black Holes and the Big Bang.

Lewis Thomas, *The Lives of a Cell: Notes of a Biology Watcher.* A gentle, elegant man, a scientist who was also a master prose stylist, here offers more insights into the world of natural sciences.

James D. Watson, *The Double Helix.* This early, classic story about the discovery of the structure of DNA offers startling insights into the workings of competitive world-class science. The author is one of the principal contenders in the field.

Gary Zukav, *The Dancing Wu Li Masters: An Overview of the New Physics.* Like the Zen masters, the author gently dances along at the reader's side, enticing him or her into the complex material, as he offers insights into the universal mysteries.

Science Fiction

Science fiction has always seemed to be a separate domain, with its own language and rulers. Not being a devotee, I would not presume to suggest books in a field that requires both knowledge and love of the books. I have wisely turned to a friend and former colleague, Ellen Asher, who, as editor of the Science Fiction Book Club and a traveler who has toured this planet meeting with other science fiction writers and fans, is the real thing, the genuine voice of authority. I defer to her suggestions both for those classic books which are *sine qua non* for anyone who wants to know the basic geography, and then for another list for those who want to be up to the minute on today's world of SF.

THE CLASSICS

Brian Aldiss, *The Helliconia Trilogy: Helliconia Spring, Helliconia Summer, Helliconia Winter.* A sweeping saga of life on a distant world whose seasons are a century long.

Isaac Asimov, *The Foundation Trilogy.* An epic saga of the fall and rise of a galactic empire. Winner of the Hugo Award for the Best All-Time Series.

Ray Bradbury, *The Martian Chronicles.* Poetic tales of a planet Mars of the imagination.

Arthur C. Clarke, *Rendezvous with Rama.* Multi-award-winning novel about the exploration of an alien space ship.

Samuel R. Delany, *Dhalgren* or *Triton.* Complex and controversial New Wave science fiction novels.

Philip K. Dick, *The Man in the High Castle.* This cult favorite of the literati tells an alternate history in which the Axis powers won World War II.

Robert A. Heinlein, *Stranger in a Strange Land.* The 1961 cult classic about a young man raised by Martians who returns home to earth.

Frank Herbert, *Dune.* The great ecological novel.

Ursula K. Le Guin, *The Left Hand of Darkness.* A remote planet whose inhabitants are of mutable sexuality. These neuter folk become male or female depending upon whom they are with.

Walter M. Miller, Jr., *A Canticle for Leibowitz.* The stirring novel of civilization's recovery following the dark age brought on by nuclear holocaust.

Gene Wolfe, *The Book of the New Sun: The Shadow of the Torturer, The Claw of the Conciliator, The Sword of the Lictor, The Citadel of the Autarch.* Coming-of-age epic in which a young apprentice-torturer is sent wandering across a strange and baroque far future *Urth.*

Roger Zelazny, *Lord of Light.* About a group who pass themselves off as Gods, using technology to dominate.

New and Noteworthy

Peter S. Beagle, *The Innkeeper's Song.* The newest novel by the author of *The Last Unicorn.*

David Brin, *Glory Season.* Genetic engineering.

Ellen Datlow and Terri Windling, eds., *Black Thorn, White Rose.* Modern takes on fairy tales.

Ellen Datlow and Terri Windling, eds., *The Year's Best Fantasy and Horror.* An annual anthology.

Gardner Dozois, ed., *Modern Classic Short Novels of Science Fiction.*

Gardner Dozois, ed., *The Year's Best Science Fiction.* An annual anthology.

David G. Hartwell and Kathryn Cramer, eds., *The Ascent of Wonder.* Huge anthology of hard science fiction including many great works.

Robert Holdstock, *Lavondyss.* If Joseph Campbell had written a novel, this would be it. A fictional journey into the origins of myth.

James Morrow, *Towing Jehovah.* A controversial and much-discussed novel. The ultimate "God Is Dead" book.

Michael Swanwick, *The Iron Dragon's Daughter.* A fantasy about a changeling in a dragon factory.

Harry Turtledove, *The Guns of the South.* What might have happened if a group of dissident South Africans had given the Confederacy several thousand AK 47s.

Connie Willis, *Doomsday Book.* A 21st-century historian is sent back to the years of the Black Plague.

Robert Charles Wilson, *The Harvest.* What happens when extraterrestrials offer humans the chance to become immortal.

Mystery

Most mystery readers know what they like. If they belong to a reading group, they may take turns from quaint cottage mysteries to P.I.s. Here are some classic mystery writers as well as some of the newer award-winners, who will be an addition or a change of pace for your reading group.

Agatha Christie, *Miss Marple: The Complete Short Stories.* The sleuth of St. Mary Mead struts her stuff.

Patricia D. Cornwell, *The Body Farm.* Sleuth Kay Scarpetta consults for the FBI serial killer unit and investigates the murder of an 11-year-old girl in North Carolina.

Elizabeth George, *Playing for Ashes.* A modern British Detective Inspector with an ever-helpful female Detective Sergeant.

Sue Grafton, *"A" Is for Alibi.* The first in her well-received alphabet series. You can go right along through the alphabet and have a good time.

Sue Grafton, *"K" Is for Killer.* The 11th in this deft mystery series; this one is about a nasty video and a young murdered prostitute.

Tony Hillerman, *Sacred Clowns* **and** *Coyote Waits.* Officer Jim Chee of the Navajo Tribal Police sorts out some dark doings out West.

Jonathan Kellerman, *Private Eyes.* A psychologist sleuth uses his highly developed intuition to solve problems.

John Mortimer, *Rumpole on Trial.* Some stories in which the famously crabby barrister outdoes himself.

Sara Paretsky, *Tunnel Vision.* Chicago private investigator V. I. Warshawski solves yet another crime.

Elizabeth Peters, *The Last Camel Died at Noon.* Archaeologist/ sleuth solves crimes in some of the best ancient settings.

Ruth Rendell, *The Crocodile Bird.* A mother and daughter caught in obsessive love, set in an isolated English manor.

Josephine Tey, *The Daughter of Time.* The mystery of Richard III: Was he or was he not the murderer of the little Princes? Reading Shakespeare's *Richard III* as background really rounds out a magnificent discussion.

Ghosts and Ghouls

Some people like to be scared. And some people like to read scary books. Those who like to have their toes curl and their hair stand on end are especially privileged to live at the same time as The King. And Stephen King is just that. He rules the horror roost by sheer dint of his amazing imagination, whose influences reach way back to when *Dracula* was a best-seller. Here are a few other books in which cleverness counts and so does talent.

Jane Austen, *Northanger Abbey.* The Great Lady's sly and most witty Gothic novel, complete with spooks in castle turrets.

Caleb Carr, *The Alienist.* Someone is murdering little boys. The setting is New York City in the 1890s; the scene is grim, the writing first-rate.

Wilkie Collins, *The Woman in White.* The Victorian best-seller featuring the nefarious Count Fosco, an insane asylum, and a fragile heiress.

Charles Dickens, *The Mystery of Edwin Drood.* His last, uncompleted novel, filled with his century's love of dark secrets.

Isak Dinesen, *Seven Gothic Tales.* The Baroness Blixen's first book (1934) includes some very elegant, phantasmagorical stories.

Ghosts, selected by Marvin Kaye. A treasury of stories, old and new, from such writers as Oscar Wilde, Isaac Asimov, Frederik Pohl, and others dedicated to chilling their readers.

Peter Hoeg, *Smilla's Sense of Snow.* More of a thriller than a ghostly tale, as a small boy's mysterious fall from a snowy rooftop begins to unravel a mystery in both Denmark and Greenland.

Henry James, *The Turn of the Screw*. The governess, the two kids, and the ghosts. Literary speculation: Did James literally believe in those ghosts, or were they merely psychic shades?

Stephen King. The Modern Master. Begin with his first novel, *Carrie* (1974), about a telekinetic wallflower, and go right on past *The Shining*. It's hard to miss with King. He is remarkably prolific and just as consistently good.

Alison Lurie, *Women and Ghosts*. Even such properly mainstream novelists as Lurie love the ectoplasmic; she struts her stuff in these wonderfully imaginative and chilly tales.

Edgar Allan Poe. The Master. Try "The Pit and the Pendulum," "The Murders in the Rue Morgue," "The Tell-Tale Heart," any of the *Tales of the Grotesque and Arabesque*. His personal disasters probably led him further out of his own reality to explore some wildly imaginative themes.

Alan Ryan, ed., *Vampires*. Who knew that those chilling creatures came in so many guises? From Victorian tales to modern stories, this spirited anthology is not for the faint of heart.

Bram Stoker, *Dracula*. The 1897 story behind all those movies reveals a strong eroticism in its tale of vampires and the power of ghoulish love.

The Age Mystique

It used to be that no woman wanted to talk about her age. Now, the best women around want to talk and write about little else. It's great to have some of these topics out of the closet. A good reading group can learn and share a lot with some of these important recent titles.

Betty Friedan, *The Fountain of Age.* It's not surprising that Friedan, who, 30 years ago, called our attention to "the feminine mystique," now views the years after 65 as a time of new freedom. An upbeat look at the gifts that getting older can offer.

Germaine Greer, *The Change.* This provocative discussion of menopause's physical and emotional effects makes a lively complement to Sheehy's book.

Erica Jong, *Fear of Fifty.* Always feisty and scrupulously candid, Jong takes a hard look at where she is, and reveals her trepidations and also her hopes for good times still to come. Nifty.

Nancy Mairs, *Ordinary Time: Cycles in Marriage, Faith and Renewal.* Some wise reflections on getting older and how the author came to accept life's passages.

Gail Sheehy, *The Silent Passage.* The psychological meaning and importance of menopause in a woman's life.

Naomi Wolf, *The Beauty Myth.* This exploration of how images of women's beauty are used against them is guaranteed to stir lively discussion.

Women's Interests

All kinds of books interest women, but in recent years some books and their authors have taken on special meaning and importance. This list includes a few of those that seem to have mattered.

Ellen Chesler, *Woman of Valor: Margaret Sanger and the Birth Control Movement in America*. A strong biography as well as a history of women's struggle for reproductive freedom.

Kate Chopin, *The Awakening*. A New Orleans wife and mother finds that the cosseted life she has known is no longer enough. A wonderful novel.

Clarissa Pinkola Estes, *Women Who Run with the Wolves*. This was probably more bought than read, though a reading group would be a helpful forum to discuss and even perhaps tap into the powerful force that the author says lurks within each woman. Grrrrr.

Susan Faludi, *Backlash*. A clarion call to alert us that there are those who would negate the forward strides of feminism.

Charlotte Perkins Gilman, "The Yellow Wallpaper." The maddening effects of a wife's confinement in body and soul.

Jamaica Kincaid, *Annie John*. A well-told tale of a young Caribbean woman's coming of age.

Maxine Hong Kingston, *Woman Warrior: Memoirs of a Girlhood Among Ghosts*. An extraordinary childhood growing up in a California Chinatown.

Doris Lessing, *The Golden Notebook*. One of those seminal novels that has, over the three decades since it was first published, meant a great deal to women searching for role models.

Adrienne Rich, *Of Woman Born.* The poet's reflections on the complex meanings of being a woman at this time.

Joanna L. Stratton, *Pioneer Women: Voices from the Kansas Frontier.* One of the first successful attempts to put together a book of writings about those remarkable women who worked hard and long to build this country.

Deborah Tannen, *You Just Don't Understand: Women and Men in Conversation.* The best-selling exploration of how the sexes differ. Some reading groups have related strongly to this one.

Twyla Tharp, *Push Comes to Shove.* The autobiography of an important choreographer and her struggles as an artist and a woman.

Naomi Wolf, *Fire with Fire: The New Female Power and How It Will Change the 21st Century.* A reappraisal of feminism and its power in the world of today and tomorrow.

Mothers and Daughters

It's amazing how many books have been written about the primal relationship of mother and daughter. Many recent books explore these special shades of family life. These books also lend themselves to exceptionally fine group discussions. Everyone, after all, has a mother.

Dorothy Allison, *Bastard out of Carolina*. Reading groups seem to love this first novel about a young girl already too old, her self-absorbed mother, and the stepfather from hell.

Evelyn S. Bassoff, *Mothering Ourselves: Help and Healing for Adult Daughters*. A compassionate psychotherapist's view of missed chances.

Hope Edelman, *Motherless Daughters*. Women prevailing after the death of their mothers.

Gail Godwin, *A Mother and Two Daughters*. Southern, of course, but universal too is this inclusive story about a widow coming to terms with her needy adult daughters.

Vivian Gornick, *Fierce Attachments*. A strong and autobiographical voice about the battle of love between a Jewish mother and her daughter.

Geeta Kothari, ed., *Did My Mama Like to Dance?* Mother-daughter is the theme of this collection by writers as varied and as talented as Amy Tan, Terry McMillan, and Barbara Kingsolver.

Susannah Moore, *My Old Sweetheart*. A lovely first novel focused on an unusual mother-daughter relationship. The book, set in fragrant Hawaii, has a wonderful sense of place.

Reflections

❧

   Some reading groups very much enjoy the shared experience of discussing issues of an ethical and moral nature. With so many new books exploring the spiritual life, readers can find a good variety to satisfy their interest in making reflection a part of daily life.

Melody Beattie, *Codependent No More.* Certainly the book that started an industry of reevaluating relationships.

Sissela Bok, *Lying: Moral Choice in Public and Private Life.* A thoughtful book about ethical dilemmas.

Betty J. Eadie, *Embraced by the Light.* The best-selling, much-discussed book about the other side of mortality.

Emmet Fox, *Power Through Constructive Thinking.* This 50-year-old guide to spiritual awareness still has insights to offer about freeing one's spirit for a more fulfilled life.

Erich Fromm, *The Art of Loving.* The humanist psychoanalyst and philosopher's enduring study of the varieties and importance of love.

William James, *The Varieties of Religious Experience.* The turn-of-the-century American philosopher's defining book, in which he discusses the reality of the unseen.

Stephen Levine, *A Gradual Awakening.* How a more contemplative life can enhance and invigorate the rest of human life.

Thomas Moore, *Care of the Soul.* The surprising best-seller in which a psychotherapist turns his attention to the value of sacredness in everyday life.

M. Scott Peck, *The Road Less Travelled.* The opening line—"Life is difficult"—signals the simplicity and sympathy in this popular book about dealing on better terms with what life has to offer.

D. T. Suzuki, *An Introduction to Zen Buddhism.* The classic guide for Westerners to gaining greater understanding of Zen as an aid to self-knowledge.

Judith Viorst, *Necessary Losses.* A wise and compassionate look at those things we shed throughout our lifetime. A wonderful book that will only be enhanced by sharing it.

The Holocaust

❦

Some readers find the Holocaust a subject too painful to explore; others want to delve into its mysteries *because* of the profundity of the material. Many of the great minds of our times have chosen this perilous subject as an occasion to explore the nature of man and the universe. Those reading group members who have confronted this often-daunting material have found the experience to be immensely satisfying on both a literary and spiritual level. There are countless excellent books written about the Holocaust; these are just a few of them.

Aharon Appelfeld, *The Age of Wonders.* If you don't know this important Israeli novelist's work, this representative novel tells of a surviving son who returns to Austria to rekindle memory and a desire for life.

The Diary of Anne Frank. It doesn't matter if you've already read this telling account of a young girl and her family's days of hiding in an Amsterdam attic. The re-reading, within a book group context, calls attention to the interrelationships, making this a new and most worthwhile experience.

Thomas Keneally, *Schindler's List.* The Austrian businessman who bought his Jewish workers' safekeeping.

Carlo Levi, *Survival in Auschwitz.* The Italian writer/philosopher's reflections on his amazing life.

Primo Levi, *The Drowned and the Saved.* His last book expresses Levi's dark concern with how the Holocaust, after its survivors no longer live, will be remembered.

Carol Rittner and John K. Roth, eds., *Different Voices: Women and the Holocaust.* Intense and personal recollections by women who survived.

Art Spiegelman, *Maus I* and *Maus II.* Cartoons featuring a mouse enacting a Holocaust story too awesome for humans. An extraordinary work.

Elie Wiesel, *Night.* A classic book about a family in a death camp and the guilt of survival. All of Wiesel's extraordinary books—among them *The Accident, The Gates of the Forest,* and *Beggar in Jerusalem*—are testaments to endurance.

"Green" Books

It's great to be green and be able to discuss important environmental issues with others who share your concern. Review these selected books and then add to them the ones that have been most significant for you.

The Best of Edward Abbey. The Arizona naturalist/philosopher called this anthology his "one-man show." Selections from his best works, such as the flawless *Desert Solitaire.*

Rachel Carson, *Silent Spring.* The now-classic book which more than 30 years ago sounded the alarm about the hazards of pesticides.

Annie Dillard, *Pilgrim of Tinker's Creek.* An uncommon sensibility and an intensely personal view of life lived close to nature's world.

Al Gore, Jr., *Earth in the Balance: Ecology and the Human Spirit.* A knowledgeable view of how our earth is doing in the last years of the 20th century, by then Senator (now Vice President) Gore.

Rupert Sheldrake, *The Rebirth of Nature.* A noted biologist reflects upon our place as humans in the natural universe.

Charles F. Wilkinson, *The Eagle Bird: Mapping a New West.* Some fine essays on the American West.

Prize Winners

Everyone loves a winner. These literati were crowned with laurels in the past few years. Use them to salt and pepper your own reading lists.

NOBEL PRIZE IN LITERATURE

1985   Claude Simon, France
1986   Wole Soyinka, Nigeria
1987   Joseph Brodsky, U.S.S.R.–United States
1988   Naguib Mahfouz, Egypt
1989   Camilo José Cela, Spain
1990   Octavio Paz, Mexico
1991   Nadine Gordimer, South Africa
1992   Derek Walcott, Trinidad–United States
1993   Toni Morrison, United States
1994   Kenzaburo Oe, Japan

PULITZER PRIZE IN FICTION

1985   Alison Lurie, *Foreign Affairs*
1986   Larry McMurtry, *Lonesome Dove*
1987   Peter Taylor, *A Summons to Memphis*
1988   Toni Morrison, *Beloved*
1989   Anne Tyler, *Breathing Lessons*
1990   Oscar Hijuelos, *The Mambo Kings Play Songs of Love*
1991   John Updike, *Rabbit at Rest*
1992   Jane Smiley, *A Thousand Acres*
1993   Robert Olen Butler, *A Good Scent from a Strange Mountain*
1994   E. Annie Proulx, *The Shipping News*

PULITZER PRIZE IN GENERAL NONFICTION

1985 Studs Terkel, *The Good War*
1986 Joseph Lelyveld, *Move Your Shadow* and J. Anthony Lukas, *Common Ground*
1987 David K. Shipler, *Arab and Jew*
1988 Richard Rhodes, *The Making of the Atomic Bomb*
1989 Neal Sheehan, *A Bright Shining Lie: John Paul Vann and America in Vietnam*
1990 Dale Maharidge and Michael Williamson, *And Their Children After Them*
1991 Bert Holldobler and Edward O. Wilson, *The Ants*
1992 Daniel Yergin, *The Prize: The Epic Quest for Oil*
1993 Garry Wills, *Lincoln at Gettysburg*
1994 David Remnick, *Lenin's Tomb: The Last Days of the Soviet Empire*

NATIONAL BOOK AWARDS FOR FICTION

1985 Don DeLillo, *White Noise*
1986 E. L. Doctorow, *World's Fair*
1987 Larry Heinemann, *Paco's Story*
1988 Pete Dexter, *Paris Trout*
1989 John Casey, *Spartina*
1990 Charles Johnson, *Middle Passage*
1991 Norman Rush, *Mating*
1992 Cormac McCarthy, *All the Pretty Horses*
1993 E. Annie Proulx, *The Shipping News*
1994 William Gaddis, *A Frolic of His Own*

NATIONAL BOOK AWARDS
FOR NONFICTION

1985 J. Anthony Lukas, *Common Ground*

1986 Barry Lopez, *Arctic Dreams*

1987 Richard Rhodes, *The Making of the Atomic Bomb*

1988 Neil Sheehan, *A Bright Shining Lie: John Paul Vann and America in Vietnam*

1989 Thomas L. Friedman, *From Beirut to Jerusalem*

1990 Ron Chernow, *The House of Morgan: An American Banking Dynasty and the Rise of Modern Finance*

1991 Orlando Patterson, *Freedom*

1992 Paul Monette, *Becoming a Man*

1993 Gore Vidal, *United States: Essays 1952–1992*

1994 Sherwin B. Nuland, *How We Die: Reflections on Life's Final Chapter*